The Wounded Pastor

The Wounded Pastor

A Healing Strategy for
Unjustifiable Termination
and Forced Resignation

by Matthew Tanner, DMin

MORLEY, MISSOURI

– an imprint of –

P.O. Box 238
Morley, MO 63767
(573) 472-9800
www.acclaimpress.com

Editor: Charles A. Francis
Book Design: Frene Melton
Cover Design: Rodney Atchley

Copyright © 2023, Matthew Tanner, DMin
All Rights Reserved.

No part of this book shall be reproduced or transmitted in any form or by any means, electronic or mechanical, including photocopying, recording or by an information or retrieval system, except in the case of brief quotations embodied in articles and reviews, without the prior written consent of the publisher. The scanning, uploading, and distribution of this book via the Internet or via any other means without permission of the publisher is illegal and punishable by law.

ISBN: 978-1-948901-85-7 / 1-948901-85-4
Library of Congress Control Number: 2021939523

First Printing: 2023
Printed in the United States of America
10 9 8 7 6 5 4 3 2 1

This publication was produced using available information.
The publisher regrets it cannot assume responsibility for errors or omissions.

CONTENTS

Acknowledgments 8
Foreword 9
Introduction 10

   chapter one: Setting the Stage 13
   chapter two: Stories from the Wounded 25
   chapter three: The Extent of the Battle 37
   chapter four: Mapping the Battlefield 43
   chapter five: Biblical Examples—Part 1 61
   chapter six: Biblical Examples—Part 2 69
   chapter seven: A New Testament Example 79
   chapter eight: Common Indicators in the Church 85
   chapter nine: Counting the Cost 93
   chapter ten: A Strategy for Healing—Economically 103
   chapter eleven: A Strategy for Healing—Emotionally 109
   chapter twelve: A Strategy for Healing—Spiritually 119
   chapter thirteen: Benefiting from Adversity 125
   chapter fourteen: For Coaches and Mentors 131

   appendix a: Written Interview Guide 139
   appendix b: Quantitative Data 143
   appendix c: Further Research and Data 149

Bibliography 158
Endnotes 164
About the Author 170
Scriptural References 172
Index 173

*Dedicated to all the pastors
who have found themselves
walking through the difficult path of
unjustified terminations and forced resignations.*

May you find healing!

ACKNOWLEDGMENTS

I would like to first thank my wonderful bride, Heather Tanner, for her wonderful support, prayers, and understanding as I journeyed through this process. I could not have walked this path without you.

I want to thank my girls, Sarah, Shelby, and Sammie. Thank you for sacrificing to allow your daddy to pursue this project, and I cannot be more proud of who God is shaping you all to be.

Thank you to my parents, Steve and Mary Tanner, and my brothers and sisters for believing in me and helping to shape me early on to arrive at this point.

Thank you to Dr. Miller for stretching me to think beyond the hurt to see the truth and for challenging my thinking every step of the way.

Thank you to Dr. Thompson for being a mentor and a friend for many years. Your contribution to this project and my ministry cannot be put into words.

Thank you to the men who took the time to share their stories of a very painful journey. Without your story the project simply would not exist.

Matthew Tanner, DMIN

FOREWORD

Have you been terminated from a ministry without sufficient Biblical reason for such a termination? Was there a power struggle that you lost in the church or ministry that you served? How does one deal with the consequences of having been terminated under such conditions? How closely does the resulting trauma align with post-traumatic stress disorder?

Having known Dr. Matthew Tanner for several years and having observed his progress in ministry as one of his professors, mentors, friends, and colleagues, I am delighted to offer this foreword for his book dealing with unjust terminations in ministry.

Dr. Tanner has experienced this phenomenon himself and those whom he interviewed for this book have also endured this experience. The objective of birthing a strategy to aid those who have been through the trials and tribulations associated with unjust terminations so that they may eventually find themselves back in the ministry has been realized. I know it is Dr. Tanner's fervent hope to aid others who have been through the kinds of experiences he has had in his ministry that can cause one to reconsider the calling to ministry. As an experienced pastor, and as one who was the youngest Associational Director of Missions in his state at one point in his journey, Dr. Tanner was uniquely qualified to conduct the research that birthed the strategy to be found in this book.

If you have experienced the trauma described in his book, I know it is Dr. Tanner's prayer and mine that the work he has done will offer you the benefits of comfort, reassurance, and a strategy for your future in ministry.

Steven H. Thompson, DMin
Associate Professor of Pastoral Ministry (Retired)
Midwestern Baptist Theological Seminary

INTRODUCTION

The world of unjustified termination and forced resignation of pastors is largely unstudied and the scope of the problem is largely unknown. The purpose of this dissertation was to create a strategy to enable pastors to fulfill their Biblical calling by successfully entering back into vocational ministry better equipped for the next assignment. The objectives of this project was to define the nature of the phenomenon, then to take a first look into the scope of the problem, and finally to seek to propose a strategy to help those pastors survive the transitionary period and re-enter ministry stronger and better equipped. This was accomplished through the phenomenological study method focusing on the lived experiences of the pastors.

I will always remember the day that I sat down at my computer to start the research for this project. I realized quickly that very little has been written specifically about pastors that are being wounded in this way by the church, yet almost weekly I hear about another brother in the Lord walking through this difficult journey. This will not be a type of book that you can simply read through once and feel as if you have mined it for its depth. This is a journey that will take you back and forth through the chapters as you seek to heal from the hurt and pain caused by being forced from a ministry that you have given your heart and life. A pastor and friend, David Thompson, explained it best when he told me that the first three or four chapters are like Luke and the rest is like Mark or Acts. I do not pretend for a moment to put this anywhere near the likes of God's Holy Word, but what David meant by this is that the first three or four chapters required a great deal of foundational work and developing a background for the reader that is necessary but much harder to walk through. Thus, as in the book of Luke, the readers needed more detail to understand what he was saying. The remaining chapters are like Mark and Acts and will flow more freely.

I asked two dear pastors and friends to read the manuscript and they agreed with the following. The point of this message is to encourage you to stay the course. The reader that takes the time to set the correct foundation in the first chapters will find it rewarding and more meaningful in the remaining chapters. Every reader will find a different character or chapter that they identify with the most and some chapters will leave no connection. That is okay because it was purposefully written this way. The main point is keep with it and my prayer is that you will find healing through none other than Christ Himself as we as wounded pastors journey together.

Dr. Matthew Tanner
A Fellow Wounded Pastor

"I have an affinity for Christ's understanding experientially what it means to be falsely accused, tried, and convicted in the kangaroo court of religious bigotry."

—A Wounded Pastor

"After they had preached the gospel to that city and had made many disciples, they returned to Lystra and to Iconium and to Antioch, strengthening the souls of the disciples, encouraging them to continue in the faith and saying, 'through many tribulations we must enter the kingdom of God.'"

(Acts 14:21–22 NASB, emphasis mine)

chapter one

SETTING THE STAGE

How Pastors Are Being Wounded in the Church

Pastor Bill had that all too familiar, uneasy feeling when he heard the knock at his office door. He had not slept much the previous evening after the phone call from John, the chairman of the deacons, asking to meet today. Maybe it was the tone in the voice, but Bill knew the battle was coming. Bill ran through all kinds of scenarios in his mind, but mostly wondering what could not wait until the regular meeting with the deacons.

As John came through the door, Bill forced a smile and said, "Morning, John. What's going on?"

"Sit down, Pastor Bill," John said after the obligatory handshake that felt cold and business-like, rather than the warm grasp he had grown accustomed to for the past six months they'd known each other. The handshake all but confirmed his suspicions—this would not be a pleasant meeting.

"The deacon board had an emergency meeting last night," John said, almost apologetically. "I guess you are aware that there has been some talk going around the congregation."

"The Bible calls that gossip," Bill said.

"I wouldn't disagree with you. It's terrible. But the sad thing is, most of the church seems to believe it." John replied.

"Most of the church? Or a handful of members who are the most vocal and seem to have power? Let me know who is leading this talk and I will go to them and see if we can resolve any issues they may have."

"That does not really matter right now. The problem is that at this point, your ability to effectively lead this church is compromised, and we've decided that we need to let you go."

At that point, Bill—unjustly terminated from his position as pastor—became a "wounded pastor." At that moment, Bill could not even think about how he was let go without just cause, or the backbiting and smear campaign that led to his termination. The only things he could think about in this moment were, "How will I pay my bills? What will I tell my wife? Will I ever pastor another church? For that matter, if this is what ministry is going to be all about, do I even want to pastor another church?"

This is a scenario that is all too familiar to many pastors. They have either had to walk through this experience themselves or have had to counsel a fellow wounded pastor who has no idea how to handle this pain. The added pain is that far too many of these Wounded Pastors are being left behind without a path forward or a way to heal. This book seeks to provide an answer to this problem.

*****

Nemo resideo: This is an unofficial combat motto of the United States Military which means no man is left behind. When in combat, our United States Military and the soldiers that make up this fighting force will do all that they can to make sure no one is left on the battlefield. The soldier may only make it home to be buried on American soil and to bring closure to their families, but they will come home. I have personally never been in military combat, and I do not pretend to know what that experience is like. However, I do have close personal friends who, as Marines, have experienced combat situations. They have relayed to me that combat can be a scary and confusing time, with the commanders barking out orders, lives in danger, the fog of war closing in, yet the soldiers remain steadfast to the mission that they have been tasked with. Somehow, in all this madness of combat, they hold true to the motto that no one is left behind on the battlefield. I believe that Evangelicalism has lost sight of this and one of the problems that we face today is we are not adhering to this motto of no one left behind on the battlefield.

We must face the painful reality that pastors are being left on the battlefield of ministry and admit that something must be done to remedy the situation. This journey you are about to undertake in the remaining chapters of this book is as follows: to define the nature of the phenomenon; measure the extent of the problem; take an honest look at the evidence of this phenomenon within Evangelical churches; speak to some common indicators that a pastor may find in the church to know if this phenomenon is about to take place; identify Biblical characters with the same experiences that fit the four quadrants of ministry, spending a complete chapter on the life of David and the stages of healing; and unveil a strategy for pastors to use in order to find strength and healing and a viable return to ministry.

The laying down of the foundation will take some time to do properly and may feel a bit harder to read through but it is vastly important to the complete understanding of the strategy that will follow. I pray you will stay the course and know that, like building a house, the work is slow at the beginning but the final product will be worth the wait.

I will refer to this phenomenon that is tearing away at the heart of the church as the unjustified termination/forced resignation of pastors.[1] Pastors know this and often speak of it anecdotally, yet before now it has not been clearly and succinctly identified, therefore, let me define this process that is affecting many pastors and church leaders in at least two ways. It is first defined as "the process by which a congregation, a personnel committee, or individual leader within a church terminates or forces a minister from a position of ministry."[2] Secondly, it is defined from the pastor's perspective as getting to the point that the pastor abdicates his post "due to the constant negativity found in personal attacks and criticism from a small faction within the congregation from whom the minister feels psychologically pressured to step down from his service of ministry."[3] These two definitions bring to light a serious problem in the hearts of our churches.

This phenomenon of pastors being forced from the pulpit has been lurking in the shadows for many years. There have been several well-done studies and surveys to ascertain the rate of pastoral exits in various denominations and even surmising as to the reasons or causes. Few have attempted to go as far as reasoning out the problem and coming up with some viable solutions to fix it or at least developing a strategy to help those affected by it. I can remember in my seminary training being told that 50 percent of the students sitting in that given classroom would not retire in the ministry. The only advice to us at the time was, "do not be the pastor who does not make it to the finish line of ministry." We were told to make sure we finished the race that was set before us, as Paul would say if he were sitting there. This is not necessarily a fault of the seminary training; however, there was no strategy given for how to navigate one of the most difficult areas of ministry so that one does not fade away from the race. Throughout my ministry I have heard men, from senior pastors to youth pastors, say that one has not truly arrived as a minister of the Gospel unless one has been fired from a church at least once. They laugh it off, yet the pain is still in their eyes and their hearts and many never fully heal.

This world of unjustified terminations and forced resignations is a forest mired in pain, hurt feelings, financial damage, bitter spouses, dying churches, and the list goes on. I have personally walked this path, and I understand the difficult journey this can be. That is why this book will attempt to finally reach into that forest to find some answers to problems that we know are there, for which little has been offered as a remedy.[4]

I chose the term *unjustified* purposefully to point to a very important distinction that is found when looking at the problem of terminations and resignations within the Evangelical Church.[5] I will seek to define the two types of terminations and resignations that occur within the church and clarify them before moving forward with Biblical examples, identify some data as to the scope of the problem, and finally point to a strategy for healing. I will use the terms *justified* and *unjustified forced termination/resignation* to outline some differences and similarities and to point to an intended scope and method of studying the phenomenon.

Is it Justified or Unjustified?

Justified forced terminations and resignations occur when pastors have either been terminated or given the singular option to resign, meaning that if they do not resign, then termination will follow, with just Biblical cause. The reasons for putting these terminations under the justified category is that the church, the one who "employs" the minister, has some viable and Biblical reason that this termination or resignation should happen. The leadership of the church can point to a chapter and verse in Scripture to say that Pastor Smith has violated the mandates of the Word of God and, therefore, can no longer continue in the capacity of pastor. The pastors who find themselves in this category include, but are not limited to, those guilty of moral failings, such as sexual or emotional affairs, or possible financial failures, such as mismanagement and/or stealing of funds. The category of justified terminations or resignations can even be as simple as not following through with a predetermined set of goals.

For example, Pastor A will complete a set number of hours of training as a predetermined set of goals that were agreed upon by both parties before the hiring event. If Pastor A does not reach the goals, then termination or resignation may happen. This work of building a strategy for pastors who have experience justified terminations and resignations is not geared for this group. Their resignations are justified, meaning with good reason, and in many cases the goal of reentry into ministry is simply not an option, especially if the moral or ethical failure was egregious enough. There are also many resources available, through written sources and counseling sources, that are directed to this group who have been justifiably removed from ministry. There is much that can and has been gleaned from interviewing these churches to see what could have been done to prevent the situation that they have experienced from occurring, however, these issues are not within the scope of this book.

Unjustified terminations and forced resignations are completely different and have in their grasp a much higher number of pastors than the category of the justified that was previously mentioned. The definition of unjustified is that there is no Biblical mandate that has been broken to cause the minister in question to be forced from the ministry position, either through forced resignation or actual termination. Simply put, the church cannot point to a chapter or verse in Scripture to state that something has been done immorally or unethically, therefore the reasons that cause this to take place are largely man's invention.

The reasons for termination and forced resignation, found within this unjustified category, are many, but I will point out a few for the sake of reference. An article in the *SBC Life* publication,[6] although admittedly not a scientific study, conducted some research as to the top reasons for unjustified terminations and resignations. Their top five reasons are, in order: 1) control issues, 2) poor people skills on the part of the pastor, 3) a pastor's leadership style being too strong, 4) the church already being in conflict prior to the pastor's arrival, and 5) the pastor's leadership style being too weak. These issues have remained in the top five steadily over the past several years while issues such as declining attendance and doctrinal issues are usually found in the number six and seven spots. It is only when one comes to the last three spots of frequency of occurrence in churches that one finds justified reasons meaning ethical or moral misconduct and dishonesty.

David Roach in his article to the Baptist Press, "Pastoral Terminations: Common but often Avoidable," states:

> "The most common causes of forced termination among Southern Baptists are 'control issues,' 'pastor's leadership style' and 'poor people skills on the part of the pastor,' according to the forced ter-

minations report. Among the top 15 causes of forced terminations, only two are related to sin by the pastor—'ethical misconduct' at no. 8 and 'sexual misconduct' at no. 10."[7]

The point of this is that when one looks at frequency of occurrence, non-justified and unbiblical reasons for termination and resignation happen at a much greater rate than for reasons that would be justified Biblically.

The most common reason for this happening that I personally have experienced is a fight over leadership and control. This happens when there is entrenched leadership within the local congregation and the minister comes in and is perceived as a usurper while seeking to exercise Biblical leadership. The ministry becomes a power struggle as to who is going to control the church, and the entrenched leadership either wins the struggle or wears down the pastor. This leadership is usually comprised of deacons, their wives, and those who have grown up in the church, have seen pastors come and go and, therefore, have arrived at a misplaced sense of ownership of the church.

Another reason for this issue can be that the pastor is simply reaching the "wrong" people or people different than the rest of the congregation. The fight can be over even the most pathetic of reasons, such as the car that the pastor drives or the way the pastor ties his tie.[8] Whatever the reason, the church either convinces itself that a termination is needed or they intentionally make life so difficult for the pastor and his family that they are forced to leave. This is what I mean by unbiblical and unjustified forced terminations and resignations.

Drawing the Complete Picture

I want to draw attention to Figure 1.1, which depicts the nature of the problem and then add some further explanation as to the definition of the problem.

The top left quadrant (Quadrant 1) shows a relationship where the church is right and pastor are acting in a Biblical manner toward each other and toward the work of the church. I understand that areas of needed improvement can be identified, and growth can always be cultivated, but the relationship is healthy. The leadership of the church, starting with the pastor, is acting in a godly manner when dealing with the pastor-church relationship and the task of leading the church. The issue of termination

Justified vs Unjustified Pastoral Termination

	Church (Employer) Right	Church (Employer) Wrong
Minister (Employee) Right	No Termination	Unjustified Termination
Minister (Employee) Wrong	Justified Termination	Mutual Termination

Figure 1.1

is not raised because the relationship is personally and Biblically healthy. Quadrant 1 is the goal of the church-pastor relationship, to have a healthy yet growing relationship between church and pastor for the sake of building the Kingdom of Christ.

The bottom left quadrant (Quadrant 2) is the relationship in which the church is Biblical in its actions and the minister is acting sinfully. This is a relationship in which the pastor or church leader has disobeyed a Biblical mandate or principle, and the church is justified in making the termination. The church will offer some sort of benevolent support for the terminated minister in the majority of these cases. Examples of the pastors and church leaders that fall into this category have come across all our paths and are a sad fact of the enemy taking out men who were in the ministry, but this quadrant does not fall within the scope of this current book. The issue in Quadrant 2 is that, as disobeying the Biblical mandate is wrong, the church is justified in the removal of the pastor, yet should seek redemptive and restorative action for the outgoing individual.

The bottom right quadrant (Quadrant 3) is what I will call the caustic relationship. This is the pastor-church relationship in which both parties are acting sinfully. The church and the minister are acting in an ungodly manner toward each other. I will illustrate this with an example from a church in Florida that I will simply call Florida Baptist Church. The pastor's leadership style was very brash, and he attempted to push the church instead of leading the church. There was nothing that was found that would be strictly against Biblical standards, such as a moral or gross ethical failure. However, the pastor would spend money without approval from the church, which led to caustic relationships within the leadership of the church. The church, reacting to the caustic nature of the pastor, responded by withholding reimbursements and acting in a way that would circumvent the pastor's leadership. Members of the church then began to position themselves in either the church's camp or the pastor's camp, and sides were formed. This caustic relationship continued for several years, to the detriment of the growth and health of the church, with the pastor ultimately moving to a different ministry setting. Although this is a brief description wrought with generalities, the fact remains that both the pastor and the church were wrong. The pastor and church at Florida Baptist Church eventually went their separate ways and the church today, with better and more godly leadership, is thriving. In the case of Florida Baptist Church, the Quadrant 3 result of mutual termination handled the problem.

This brings us to the final quadrant (Quadrant 4), which is the unjustified termination quadrant and is the heart of this book. In Quadrant 4, the pastor is right and the church is acting incorrectly. This is not to say that the pastor is perfect and has not made any mistakes in leadership, but the pastor in Quadrant 4 has not disobeyed any Biblical mandate or principle. This is the case in which the church or congregation, or other actors and factions within the church, are pushing for the removal of the pastor by either termination or forced resignation. The actions against the pastor are for reasons other than moral or ethical failure, and no clear Biblical mandate or principle exists to support their reasons. The reasons the church gives for the termination can be anything from not liking the preaching style, to reaching the wrong people, to making the "real" leaders in the church angry, to any "reason" the group can invent. The pastors in this category are unjustly pushed out or removed from their leadership positions due to the sinfulness of the church and their sinful reasons and resulting sinful actions. Quadrant 4 contains the tens of thousands of ministers who have been unwittingly thrust in the club of "finally making it as a minister because I have been fired from a church" or those who have resigned rather than face the continual and mounting pressure any longer.

The challenge with the understanding of how pastors are being wounded in this way is getting to the heart of the story. The reality is that the numbers and types of various reasons that a church can come up with for forced terminations in this category seem to be mind-boggling and without end. An article in the *SBC Life* journal compiled some of the main categories, which are, in order: control issues, poor people skills on the part of the pastor, the pastoral leadership being too strong, the church already in conflict before the arrival of the new pastor, the pastoral leadership being too weak, and decline in attendance. These reasons held the top six spots for the last sixteen years. Issues such as doctrinal differences and ethical and moral failures are not found until the last three spots on the top ten reasons.[9]

During the course of the study, I have been asked many times why I would not interview the churches themselves to find out what they are doing and why some continue to treat pastors this way. The difficulty with interviewing the churches that these pastors have come from is that much of the information that can be gleaned is in the nature of the unjustified and sinful reasons that led to the termination or resignation in the first place. It is my opinion that the information gleaned from the churches themselves will not lead to helping the strategy to a great degree due to the nature of the unjustified reasons. This does not mean that no attempt should be made to survey the churches at some basic level to support the interviews of the pastors and glean some useful information pertinent to the goals of this book. Knowing what drives these churches and their subsequent actions can be an integral part of a comprehensive solution. There is also the maxim that there can be truth found in every situation. Even though the churches are in the "wrong," category they may have some valid points to bring to the table, which would help pastors minimize mistakes that compound an already unstable situation.

The pastors in this category must also learn to look beyond the hurt, the fog of war, to see what they could have done differently and even to ask themselves if the situation could have been avoided. This is the proverbial getting the log out of their own eye. The interview, or storytelling process employed at the heart of this book, was much like a military debrief that takes place after a battle in which one takes an honest look at every action that took place before the battle, during the battle, and after the battle, to see what could have been done differently. This is the very crux of the challenge found in this book and in the pastor interview process used in gaining the information.

The prevailing question is whether or not enough information can be gleaned from the pastor's perspective in order to have a complete view of the problem. It is my opinion that the answer to this question is yes. I personally have been rightfully challenged along the way to look beyond my personal hurt and anger to see what I could have done better and differently, and it is not a task easily done, but in my opinion, it is possible. It is not easy, but it is possible to get the right information from those who have been through the battle. It is my opinion that the best way of reaching the heart of the issue and devising a viable strategy is to hear the stories of the men who are victims of this phenomenon[10] and find the strategy that lies within.

When pastors have a road map to follow and a community of support, it is possible for them to again enter ministry stronger than they were before. The atmosphere in many churches today is causing shepherds to be wounded in the ministry, and it is time the healing begins! The next chapter will share the stories of three pastors who were made to walk this path, along with a brief synopsis of my own story, to begin to show the hurt that unjustified termination and forced resignation causes pastors and their families.

Pastor, as you read this book, I want to encourage you to stay the course. The strategy you are looking for is coming. This phenomenon must be first clearly defined to add necessary weight to the strategy at the end. I know that you will be rewarded at the end of this journey with hope and healing. My prayers are with you as we travel this journey now before us.

"I must say that God has brought me through this, has healed my hurt, but occasionally Satan sends darts of remembrance and I hurt for a moment, but then the healing returns."
—*A Wounded Pastor*

chapter two

STORIES FROM THE WOUNDED

I am currently serving, at the time of writing this chapter, as the interim pastor of a small church in rural Southeast Missouri. I have been on this ministry field for approximately a month-and-a-half as I am writing this chapter. Prior to this assignment, I was away from full-time vocational ministry due to experiencing a forced resignation. The current church is a rural church set in a small bedroom community of about 2,000 residents. This area of ministry is what I consider an over-churched and under-reached area of Southeast Missouri, with approximately twenty churches in a ten to fifteen-mile radius. Five of those local churches are Southern Baptist denominationally. It is an underreached area in that many of the churches are in the small category and employ bi-vocational pastors. The church has been without a pastor for the past two years, and upon arriving on the ministry field, I found a discouraged congregation. They were beginning to feel as if they would not be able to find a pastor. The goal of the interim time is revitalizing the church and setting a vision for the future.

During the year away from ministry, I was unemployed for a period of time and worked in a secular field for the remainder of the year, and there were times when I wondered whether or not ministry would happen again, either full-time or bi-vocationally. Once a ministry assignment became forthcoming, I began to wrestle with the fear of repeating the past. Questions of the church's trustworthiness and my ability to complete the task of pastor and leader of the church began to surface. I also struggled with the pride of not wanting to be in a rural setting and the sin of wondering if I was settling for just any ministry or if this was the only way back into the field. These are the very struggles that will be dealt with in the heart of the strategy and begin to delve into what a pastor deals with in returning to ministry after a termination/resignation has taken place.

My Story—A Victim of Forced Resignation

The call from the Lord to my last church, that I will call First Baptist Church, Anytown, USA, was clear even though I had faced forced resignation in the past. The pastor search process was the same process that I have personally been through several times: The search team promised that they wanted a strong Biblical leader, the deacons wanted training on how to properly conduct the office and ministry of the deacon, and they pledged their commitment to follow the new pastor of the church. They filled the meetings with promises of great things to come when I arrived on the field. The landscape, although not perfect, seemed a welcome place to do ministry. The "in view of a call," as Southern Baptists title the preview and interview weekend, went well with a final vote reaching near 98 percent. I was very grateful to be back in the local church pastorate when I received this call that I still believe came from the Lord even though it would end as one of my most painful experiences. I felt as though I had learned from the past experiences in ministry and that I had done due diligence in asking questions of the pastor search team. I discovered that they had some difficulty in the past with a youth director and Calvinism and had had to ask the youth director to leave the church. I explored this issue as best I could; I felt comfortable that this was a singular issue not to be repeated and felt as if the Lord was leading me to this church. However, I learned quickly that I failed to notice some very sinful undertones and controlling spirits within some of the lay leaders of the church.

The grace period or honeymoon after arriving on the field, the time when everyone in the church remains happy with their "choice" of pastor, lasted approximately six weeks. It was then that I realized that the whole process of the interview and the promises made to me as pastor and to my family had been a front. I had been told what they had wanted me to hear. I must say that in the defense of the chairman of the search team, I believe that he wanted change and healing to take place. Unfortunately, he left the church before the real battle began and thus hastened the downfall. In theory and on paper, I was the pastor of this church. However, in practice, I was allowed to remain pastor if I conformed to the entrenched leadership of the church, both formal and implied leadership. I even had one deacon tell me, "Boy, you need to figure out how we do things around here!" I knew then that I was in trouble.

The six-month mark also included a critical mistake on my part. I was teaching a Bible Training Center for Pastors course in the local association and we had been discussing dual prophecy. I was very excited about the truths that were being taught, and I mentioned one of these truths to a church member in Sunday School, and it was overheard by the teacher of the class. I ignored the fact that the class would not have the correct context to understand the difficulty of the teaching, and looking back, I should have discussed it as a private conversation. I mistakenly thought everyone would want to know and would understand some of the deeper things of Scripture. I was unaware of the immaturity of the individual who challenged me regarding this point, and this created a controversy that would arise again several times in the three-and-a-half years I pastored this church. To make matters worse, it was a deacon and his wife who were at the center of this issue. I began to try to lead through these issues and make some needed changes to the church to grow and move forward, but I was met with difficulty by the deacon body at every step of the way.

This battle lasted off and on for three-and-a-half years. I began to dread deacons' meetings and business meetings because I knew they would be a fight and I would be under attack. Yet another critical mistake that I made at this assignment was not asserting authority in areas such as the business meetings and deacons' meetings from day one. I can only guess at this point that this would have changed the situation, but I do know I may have had a fighting chance to lead through the battles had I been in a better position of leadership. The issues continued, manifesting themselves in several ways, before culminating in rumors from a deacon and church member concerning my marriage being circulated throughout the community. I endured times periods all-out attacks from church members, especially at business meetings and deacons' meetings, being confronted in the hallways of the church before and after services, and continual mounting pressure. It got to the point that I would not let my family attend anything but the actual worship services and I even began to question my call to the ministry.

It was on a Monday morning, before a business meeting on the following Wednesday, that I sat at the desk in my home and opened the Bible. I told the Lord that I would stay or go, but I needed to know what was required of me. I needed Biblical proof to undergird this battle I was about to undertake in just two days. I was led by the Lord to the book of Acts to see how Paul handled this very situation in his ministry. I clearly remember sitting at the desk at my home and reading the two occasions in which Paul left a ministry under duress. In the first instance Paul shook the dust off his feet and simply moved on. The second incident was felt much closer to the situation I found myself in. In Acts, Paul was being oppressed and slandered by the people. When this oppression, which carries the meaning of an army encamping around you for the purpose of attack, and slander began to take place and Paul shook out his garment, declared the guilt to be on the heads of the attackers, and moved on from that city. I took this as God's command to leave this ministry, which I resigned from instead of waiting to be terminated, a process that I found out was already in motion.

I want to take some time now to share four key areas of my journey that will become the heart of the strategy that will develop at the end of this book. Those areas of concentration are economic issues, emotional healing, spiritual healing, and leadership development.

Economically, I moved from this pastorate through a journey of retracing some steps through some difficult areas I had lived, trying to sell a house from the previous ministry location, seeking secular employment for the first time since just after college, and wondering how we would make ends meet. I did not know at the time that I was embarking on a journey that would have me away from ministry for approximately one year. I ended up taking a hospitality position in the popular vacation destination, Branson, and moving my family in with my parents for several months. I eventually moved back into ministry first on an interim basis and at the publishing of the book I have become their permanent pastor.

Emotionally, I did not do a whole lot of healing at first. The situation that I found myself in caused me to be stuck in the economic category, which is something that will be discussed later. It was much later, after moving to an interim pastorate position that I was able to connect with a counselor and friend and walk through some emotional healing. I found quickly that I could not do this alone.

Spiritually, it was during this time that I had to relearn to love the church at large, knowing that some of its individual congregations had hurt me and my family deeply. I did not attend church at first but eventually found a place to simply sit at the back pew and be an attender. It was here that I was able to finally have some honest conversations with the Lord and begin spiritual healing.

Leadership Development lessons were somewhat slower in arriving and had I not journaled this time would have been harder to nail down. I have become a vastly different leader. I have been able to identify some weaknesses, developed new strengths largely due to the fact that my current church is very understanding of my journey. I lead through consensus and attempt to communicate better. I tend to choose battles more wisely and try to confront issues early on before they can fester into bigger battles. I have also moved more quickly to a plurality of leadership to avoid leading alone. I wish I had more to put here but I am still in discovery mode in this part of the healing strategy.

You Are Not Alone in This! Three Other Stories:

Pastor #1

Pastor #1's first church, while he was attending seminary, had been one that was mired in conflict. He had seen his position go from full-time to part-time due to the conflict and the fact that the givers of the church had withheld the tithe so that his salary would be cut in half and he would be relegated to part-time. This church eventually closed its doors, and he moved to his second pastorate, believing that he had learned valuable lessons, starting with how to walk through the search process. He went into his second church with a list of requirements that were needed, such as finishing seminary, fulfilling obligations with the National Guard, and living in a home that he already owned thirty minutes from the church instead of moving into the parsonage. It was very soon in the process that he noticed that this church had a controlling deacon who insisted on meeting him separately from the search team's process. The deacon threw a fit over the terms of the search process to the point that the certain requirements were added to the deal, such as having to pay for his own pulpit supply while away on National Guard duty. Early in the pastor's tenure the controlling deacon began to complain when money was spent on things that he did not "approve of," such as gas money for the church van.

This all came to a head around the first-year mark of this pastor's ministry at the church. He had restructured some committees, which was met with pushback on the part of the controlling deacon. The issue of the parsonage was brought up again. Although the pastor had agreed during the search process, begrudgingly, to move into the parsonage, he had not done so, mainly because he had not sold his home. The parsonage issue became a major issue with this deacon. This started about five or six weeks of battle over control and leadership of the church, which culminated in a confrontation between the pastor and the deacons. The issue was brought before the church as a vote, and only six people voted against allowing the pastor to remain in leadership and stay in the home that he owned.

This did not stop the attacks from happening. The controlling deacon took every opportunity to criticize the pastor about everything from the way he visited church members to the way he was preaching. During this time frame the pastor started keeping a record of families that stated they would attend this church if this deacon was not a member. The number rose to twenty-seven families who would not attend this church because of how this deacon had acted in the past. The last major attack was over the church's Vacation Bible School, where the controlling deacon was working behind the scenes to make sure certain positions would be unfilled, which would in turn make the pastor look bad.

The pastor was worn down to the point that he saw resignation as the only way to resolve the problems and stop the attacks on his ministry. He asked for a severance, but it was not given. The church held the meeting to vote on the pastor's resignation in a manner that was not consistent with the bylaws, and anyone who would have supported the severance was not informed of the meeting.

Economically, the pastor relied on his National Guard pay, a part-time job at Applebee's, and some scholarships that he had received for his seminary training. Emotionally the pastor attempted to heal by simply resting and being away from the attacking stress, spending a lot of time reading key books, and taking advantage of a program offered by Samford University dealing with ministry reconciliation. It was through this program that he was given the resources to go away for a week to heal as a couple and a family. At one point, he even sold plasma so that he could pay the bills in the interim time. Spiritually, this pastor simply worked to get over the bitterness at the church but also directed toward the Lord. He spent time reading through the Bible from start to finish, even when his heart was not in it. The pastor was at a point after the emotional healing and spiritual healing, able to take an in-depth look at his leadership development and discern what he could have done better in the process, learning to be less academic and to not be a people pleaser. The biggest leadership lesson for him was learning to take positions of leadership out of faith and not fear. The last lesson on leadership was for him to develop a solid, written-out theory of leadership for his life and ministry.

Pastor #2

He took his second pastorate position, his first ending in a resignation with conflict involved, even though another well-trusted pastor gave him the advice to not take this position. This church had a reputation for having conflict. The first year or so was a typical honeymoon period in which things seemed to be going well. The church now had a young pastor and a young associate pastor, even though the median age of the congregation was fifty-five and older. When the age dynamic of the congregation began to get younger, the problems and conflict began to show. The pastor admitted in the interview that he ignored some of those who wanted things to move slowly and pushed ahead with some changes.

Then an issue of church discipline arose within the church that involved a member of the church who had moved her husband out of the home and moved another man in. The pastor attempted to work through the Matthew 18 process up to the point of bringing the matter before the church. It was at this point that he was informed by one of the deacons that "church discipline may be in the Bible, but it is not for this church."

This pastor also experienced conflict with the deacon leadership in the church with one controlling deacon, also the check signer, refusing to sign the associate pastor's check because this deacon did not vote for the raise that the pastors had received that year. The conflict came to a head over what should have been a minor issue that was allowed to spiral out of control. The pastor and associate had, in an attempt to liven up the Western-themed Vacation Bible School this particular year, each dressed up as cowboys with a couple of guns strapped to their belts. These guns did not work anymore, yet it was an opportunity for controversy in the church and rumors to run rampant about what the staff had done.

There was another incident in which some of the young people in the church wanted to start new ministries but were blocked by the older congregation because "it had been tried before and did not work then, so it will not work now." The pastor was eventually confronted by the deacons about the way he was doing the invitation at the end of the service, demanding answers as to why people were not getting saved, and it must be due to his ineptness in ministry. This led to a confrontation within the deacons meeting concerning his ministry at the church. At one point, while visiting one of the deacon's ailing wives in their home, he was called the worst pastor they had ever had.

The constant attacks led this pastor to be completely worn out with ministry, and after three years of ministry at this position and through the counsel of reading God's Word, he decided that he had to resign instead of facing more of this pressure and attacks. He described his state at the time as being tired of the fight, tired of trying to reconcile with a controlling deacon who was creating problems behind the pastor's back, tired of the sleepless nights—he was simply done. The church gave him a severance of one week's pay.

Economically, he went back into construction, taking remodeling jobs as they came up. He and his wife were forced to take out a loan to pay the bills, which almost eight years later he is still paying off. At this time, he had a wife and three kids, including a newborn, to take care of. He had other pastors call him to do pulpit supply so that he could make some extra money. This pastor also stated that there was no assistance or program that he could find to help him and his family economically through this time.

Emotionally, this pastor found that he did not truly begin to heal from the hurt of the last assignment until he found another pastorate, which proved to be a loving congregation that has supported him through the healing process. The love of another church helped him to grow and love the church again. The main area that he stated was the most difficult to heal was to not be cynical toward the church.

Spiritually, this pastor increased the discipline of reading God's Word and praying through the interim time. He has kept this discipline of prayer and reading the Word with his family into his next assignment, which he credits as being a catalyst for this assignment being successful. He also made sure to attend healthy churches while looking for another ministry assignment and preached whenever the opportunity arose to keep the gift fresh.

In leadership development, this pastor has learned that he must trust and believe that not every church is the same. He has learned to be more patient when it comes to issues that arise within the church. He also learned, albeit the hard way, the importance of relational equity when it comes to leading the church and congregation. He has sought to first learn before change can occur. When asked why he was successful at this new assignment and why the cycle had been broken, he simply stated that it is because this new church loves him and he has learned to love them in return.

Pastor #3

By the time that he accepted the call as the worship pastor at his last assignment, this pastor had some experience in music development and teaching. His first ministry assignment was in the church where he grew up when a possible internship turned into a job offer as an associate to the worship pastor. This position was not without conflict as he was asked to resign by the worship pastor without the knowledge of the senior pastor. It was several years later that the worship pastor was removed for having an affair. This was simply chalked up as a learning experience, and this pastor would soon find himself as the worship arts director for a church with a seeker-sensitive model and a pastor with some musical training.

Soon after starting the position, his wife was brought on as his worship arts assistant, and even though there was a history of couples in this position not working out very well, they seemed to find a good fit and to make it work. However, after some time in the position, tension began to develop between the pastor, who was very image-driven, and the worship pastor, who was very development-driven. They seemed to be able to talk through their problems and challenges because the pastor had told them that he did not want simple yes-men.

The tension escalated when, in one of their weekly service planning meetings, the worship pastor was challenged by the lead pastor concerning some decisions that had been made. This caused the worship pastor to have to defend his philosophy of worship ministry. The pastor went on vacation not too long after this tense meeting, and when he returned, he informed the worship pastor that he would be terminated immediately. Both he and his wife were asked to leave quietly and not cause any problems. When asked for the reason for the termination, the pastor would only say a difference in philosophy. The rest of the church was not given any reason as to why they were dismissed. The pastor stated, and even wrote down in a letter, that no Biblical mandate was ignored or no gross insubordination was happening. They just simply had a difference in philosophy, and that was enough to remove them from ministry.

Economically, he has gone back to delivering truck parts, which is paid by the job. They were given a three-month severance, which has since run out. He has picked up teaching private music lessons and has been able to fill in for other worship pastors a couple of times. He, like the others, was not able to find any economic help that is available to ministers who find themselves in this position.

Emotionally, this pastor stated that healing has not happened yet and is something that he is still working on since at the writing of this project he has only been out of the ministry now for about four months. Emotional healing has taken a back seat to financial survival.

Spiritually, he has tried to grow through listening to podcasts while delivering parts at his job. He and his wife have found a church to attend to start the process of spiritual healing while looking for a new ministry position.

Leadership development is a slow process as of now due to the fact that this incident happened not that long ago, but this pastor described growth in areas of communication, being able to move from argument to compassion, working on gentleness in his approach to others, and learning to choose which battles are worthy of fighting. This as well, per this pastor, is a work in progress because the wounds are still fresh.

The reason that I share these stories is to show that I, and others, have walked the path that many pastors have traveled in the realm of forced resignation/termination. I understand the thoughts, fears, challenges, and difficulties that come with this journey. It is this understanding that has led to this project and the hopes of finding a solution to the problem.

The difficulty in studying this phenomenon is getting to the heart of how frequently this is happening in Evangelical churches. Just how many pastors are there that have stories just like the ones you have just read? The answer is that it is difficult to nail down, but it is happening way more than one might think. We now turn our attention to finding the answer to this question and defining the scope of the problem pastors are facing in church ministry today.

"It is a stain on the bride of Christ when the neighborhood near a church says, 'Oh you're the pastor now? You won't be there long!' Then the church is doing more harm than good."
—A Wounded Pastor

chapter three

THE EXTENT OF THE BATTLE
How Prevalent is the Phenomenon?

The most unfortunate reality is that the stories that I relayed to you in Chapter 2, my story and the three others, are not uncommon journeys. There are far too many pastors and church leaders who are experiencing the phenomena of forced terminations or forced resignations for unjustified and unbiblical reasons, and sadly this type of event is being played out again and again in our churches. While conducting research on the scope of the problem and searching for the prima facie case evidence for this project, I contacted two denominational leaders, and they informed me that the evidence of this problem is predominantly hearsay evidence. The studies that would produce this evidence have yet to be done, and hard statistical data simply does not exist. It is with this in mind that I will relate what has been found in research to date.

Thomas Powell, in his thesis, "Forced Terminations Among Clergy: Causes and Recovery," relates that in 2006 approximately 680 full-time and bi-vocational pastors were forced out of their ministry positions, as were 265 staff members. The numbers were larger in 2005, approximately 1,302.[12] I have also discovered that this is a global phenomenon, finding statistics from countries all over the world in which pastors are experiencing forced terminations and resignations.

The next question that must be addressed is whether the numbers have changed in the last since then. The latest study at the time of writing, conducted by Lifeway Research Group, states that 1 percent of pastors leave their ministry prematurely each year.[13] Wilson and Hoffman's work *Preventing Ministry Failure* tells us that 25 percent of clergy have been forced out or fired from ministry at least once.[14] All of the research conducted thus far shows a rise in the phenomenon of forced terminations and forced resignations within the last several years. Another study, conducted in 2012, found that three pastors leave the church every day.[15] The fact is that the problem is getting worse.

The research also shows clearly that the phenomenon is no respecter of denominations or locations with the numbers being similar, approximately 4-5% of pastors per year throughout all Evangelical denominations,[16] and reports dealing with such research throughout the global church. When all the data was compiled from these several research studies, it became clear that churches have been forcing out tens of thousands of ministers each year, across denominational lines, and the clear majority of those terminated are never returning to ministry. So much for no man left behind.

As was previously stated, the causes for the forced resignations or terminations can be as numerous as the people that make up the congregations in our church. There are always the surface issues that the churches present as the problem, and the challenge is getting to the heart issues and the root causes. The team at the School of Leadership Studies at Regent University in a working paper, "Forced Pastoral Exits: An Exploratory Study," compiled research from several sources, listing six basic categories that precede a forced exit. These categories are conflicting visions within the church, personality conflict with others in leadership or the congregations, interpersonal incompetence, unrealistic expectations, a lack of church discipline, or contentious individuals and power groups.[17]

The part of the phenomenon that is being missed is that a great portion of those that are being forced from the ministry, some numbers as high as 65%, are no longer going back into the ministry and instead seeking employment in a secular field. The pastors who do make it back into ministry are often dealing with the aftermath of the previous ministry situation and the trauma of the battle that caused the exit. I have termed this experience as post-traumatic spiritual stress disorder and will detail steps to heal from this in the chapter on emotional healing strategy. Chuck Wickman, in his work on pastors at risk, stated the lasting results that a pastor may feel after a forced resignation or termination in this way:

> "… physical, spiritual, emotional loss of energy; growing cynicism about personal value in the ministry; increasing apathy regarding ministry; going through the motions of ministry; perception that trust is turning to suspicion; tendency to withdraw from situations involving stressors; more impatience with congregations; loss of a sense of humor; increased callousness toward people; feelings of helplessness to change or break free from being overwhelmed."[18]

This shows that those who do make it back into a ministry position are facing even more difficult odds of ministry success and longer tenure because they must overcome and heal from the previous situation. Pastors, who have experienced this type of termination or resignation, have reported that they have difficulty trusting people, increased financial strain that has carried over into a new assignment, a loss in self-confidence as a leader, and severe strain on their marriages and family life. The School of Leadership at Regent University, in their 2005 study mentioned previously, also stated that of the 108 pastors they interviewed, 21% had been forced from a ministry more than once. This study further reveals that many pastors are simply taking the hurt and the forced resignation and termination ministry baggage into the next assignment, making it even harder to be successful. Pastors simply carry the problems from a previous assignment into the next assignment and, due to a lack of a healing and strengthening strategy, find themselves being forced out a second or even a third time or leaving the ministry for good. It is a very sad day when secular employment is desired over ministry because it is simply safer.

There is also another crisis that this phenomenon is creating. There are increasingly fewer men who are desiring to go into the pastorate due to the strain and difficulty that they are seeing other ministers go through. Those who are answering the call to ministry are choosing roles different than the role of pastor. When we combine the thousands of ministers who are dropping out of ministry and turning to secular work with the shortage of those who desire to go into the ministry, we are creating a shortage of church leaders. If we do not see a change in the problem of forced terminations and resignations or at least create a way for the pastors to return to ministry in a healthy manner, I am afraid that we will have empty pulpits and thus empty churches.

There are many who have noticed and reported the problem, but few are seeking a solution. Many churches are leaving broken and hurting pastors in their wake. A participant in a study conducted by Robert Elkington in his work, "Adversity in Pastoral Leadership," had this to say, "There are two main sources of adversity: the world and the visible church. The ruling paradigm for ministry simply does not work in a chaotic and post Christian world, where possibly most of your enemies are sitting in the pew."[19]

What Do I Hope to Accomplish?

This book, as stated in the previous chapters, will define the problem, giving much needed clarity as to exactly what this event is that we are talking about. Then I will give some Biblical examples of the four quadrants of termination which will help guide the discussion of the phenomenon and move to some quantifiable data as to what we know about the frequency of the problem. When an issue is only anecdotally known, time needs to be spent outlining the problem. The reward that awaits the patient reader will be a strategy to help those pastors survive the transitionary period and reenter ministry stronger and better equipped. This will be a multifaceted strategy that deals with all the areas that a pastor faces when forced from a ministry position either through forced resignation or termination.

I want to give the reader the components of the strategy upfront to guide and encourage perseverance. The first tier of the strategy will be practical in nature. Pastors who find themselves in this position must now deal with income assistance during an interim period, possibly relocating their homes due to church-owned living arrangements, finding interim employment in a secular area to sustain their families, and even down to putting themselves back into the pastor search world of résumés and search teams. This first tier of the strategy will help pastors wade through the minefield of practical issues that must be dealt with to take even the first step in a healing process.

The next two tiers of the strategy will be emotional and spiritual healing. I have already mentioned above some of the internal struggles that pastors deal with, such as trust and confidence issues. The reality is that unless pastors heal from the hurts and struggles created from their most difficult situations, they will reenter another ministry handicapped, which will often cause unnecessary issues in their next ministry because of the baggage they have brought with them.

The final tier of the strategy will be that of leadership development growth potential. It is the hope of this book to develop a way for the pastors, once they have navigated through the fog of war, to be able to take an honest look at their own situation and leadership styles to determine what changes need to be made. This is the proverbial removing the log from one's own eye. Even in the situations when the church was completely unjustified and at fault, the pastors can and should learn leadership lessons that will make the pastors stronger as pastors and teachers.

The main purpose and goal of this book is to begin to create a strategy to enable pastors to fulfill their Biblical calling by successfully entering back into vocational ministry, better equipped for the next assignment, but first we must identify the problem and call it out for what it is, a danger lurking in our churches.

Conclusion

While beginning this project, I have come across several studies, some of which are mentioned above, that bring attention to the fact that there is a problem. However, the few studies conducted thus far stop short of giving a solution to the problem or a strategy to assist the fallen soldiers of ministry. This project is attempting to accomplish this mission. There must be a strategy in place that the fallen and injured pastors and leaders can turn to for guidance and healing. Unfortunately, that is the only scope of this project. It would be a far greater undertaking to find a solution to why this is happening and to attempt to curb the frequency in our churches. The topic of decreasing the phenomenon of forced resignations and terminations in our churches must wait for another day or another project. In order to truly adhere to the idea of no man left behind, we must begin to think in terms of keeping these men in ministry and helping them to become stronger and better equipped for the increasingly difficult challenges of ministry. Scripture makes it clear that, as we draw closer to the return of our Lord and Savior, this world will become more and more difficult. The church will have its hands full in dealing with an increasingly lost and hostile world. We need ministry leaders who can stay the course and finish the race that the Lord has laid out before them. This book will help complete that mission. The next chapter will turn to investigating the evidence and quantifiable data that has been discovered this far and understanding what the trends mean to today's Evangelical pastors.

"I came to what was presented as a healthy, happy, growing congregation."

—A Wounded Pastor

"My offenses were things like taking the order of service out of the bulletin, moving a coat rack, moving the church offices, wanting to know more of what committees were doing. I was accused of changing the church by-laws that were changed by a committee and voted on by the entire church without dissent. There was no accusation of immoral or unethical actions."

—A Wounded Pastor

chapter four

MAPPING THE BATTLEFIELD
There Are Some Trends and Facts that Begin to Emerge

The goal of the journey was to gather the lived experiences of those who have walked this path while detailing some of the data that was found. This chapter will seek to analyze this information and wrestle with some of the quantifiable data to determine what it may teach the church today, considering the stories received, and to develop a strategy in the four areas of concern: economic recovery, emotional healing, spiritual healing, and leadership development.

The plan was to develop a simple, straightforward approach to a phenomenological exploration of the topic of unjustified termination and forced resignation of pastors and church leaders. I have already explained how the interviews were conducted in the previous chapters and will show in later chapters how they developed into the beginning of a strategy. I will now turn to the quantifiable data that was developed as part of the writing of this book. However, I believe it is helpful to know how the information was gathered in order to read the data in its intended context.

Direct Measurements

During the interview process, I asked each pastor I interviewed nine quantifiable data questions regarding each event they experienced. The results are detailed through the following charts. I have chosen to deal with only the most pertinent charts and data for the greater understanding of the impact of the phenomenon placing three of them in Appendix C for those who wish to see the complete data. For the purpose of data acquisition, each individual experience with the phenomenon of unjustified forced termination or resignation was termed an "event" due to the fact several of the individuals interviewed had experienced the phenomenon multiple times and were allowed to detail each event separately. Each event took place at a separate church with different locations and situations.

Here are the results:

Question One: What was your level of education when the event took place?

The first chart (Figure 1) dealt with the level of education each participant possessed at the time of the unjustified forced termination or resignation. The results of the data demonstrated that being forced from a ministry is no respecter of educational levels. Approximately 86 percent (22 out of the 30) of the individuals interviewed held a master's degree or higher, with just over 13 percent holding a doctoral degree.

This data indicates that the pastoral educational system may be lacking in preparing pastors sufficiently, especially in areas that may cause or effect the occurrence of this phenomenon. Only so much can be packed into pastoral education in the time that the student has, unless a 200-hour Master of Divinity is possible. Still, more must be done to prepare pastors through the educational medium for the difficulties they will face, and this must become a priority because of the perception that this is happening in our churches

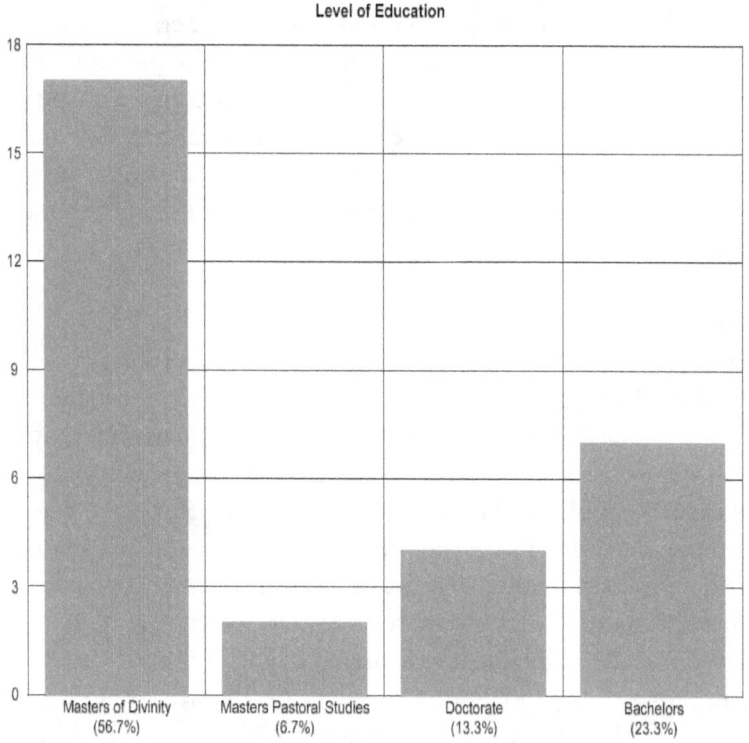

Figure 1

at such an alarming rate. The question is whether more can be done educationally to prepare these men in the areas of conflict management (especially dealing with antagonists in the church); misplaced, misdirected, or wrongly assumed leadership; and the ever-changing landscape of the church.

Question Two: How many years of ministry experience did you have when the event took place?

The second chart (Figure 2) asked the pastors how many years of ministry experience they had when the event took place in the hope of finding out whether pastoral experience helped to alleviate the instances of forced terminations and resignations that were unjustified. The question was attempting to discern whether this was a rookie leadership issue or whether it pointed back to an intrinsic problem within the church. The data was very revealing.

The first observation is that this phenomenon is scattered throughout all categories of ministry experience and can happen at any time during

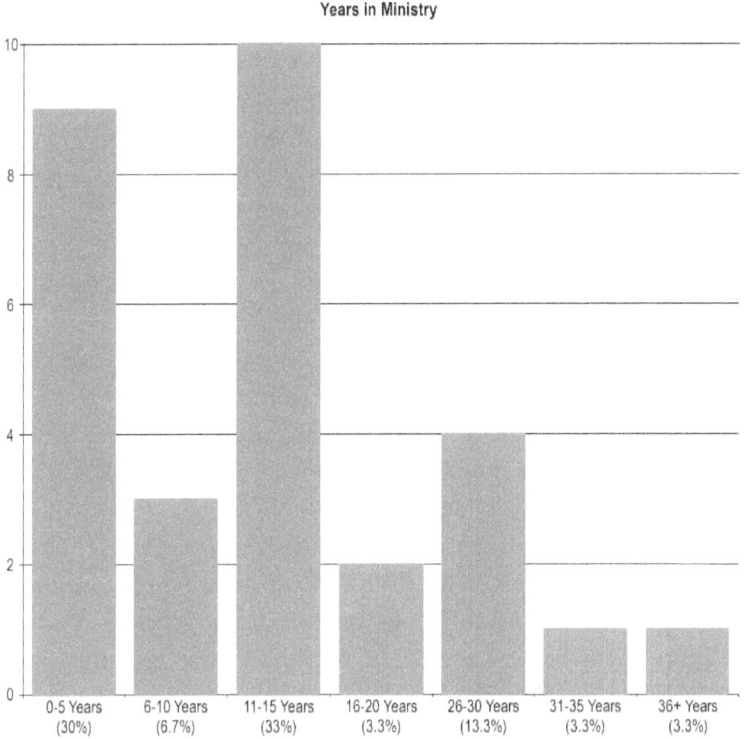

Figure 2

a pastor's career in ministry. Eight out of the thirty events happened in the more seasoned years of ministry, fifteen years and beyond, when one would assume leadership style was refined and understanding of calling was clear, all of the things that one would think would not be contributors to the phenomenon. The two largest categories in which the unjustified and forced termination or resignation took place were the 0-to-5-year mark and the 11-to-15-year mark. I was surprised to find that the highest category was not the first five years in the ministry but in fact was the 11-to-15-year category. Clearly, this is not a rookie phenomenon or young leadership issue that only happens to pastors who are green and unseasoned in the ministry nor is it more prevalent at the other end of the spectrum, happening only to well-seasoned pastors who are more established in their ways and potentially unwilling to change. Most of the instances in which the phenomenon was found were in the central years of the pastoral ministry career when one would assume the leader should be confident and more comfortable in leadership style yet still teachable.

One possible objection to the data is whether the interviewed pastors had simply misread the calling to the pastorate. It is my understanding that this cannot be so because if the pastor was fulfilling the wrong calling or simply was not really called in the first place, then one would assume the phenomenon would occur much more often in the beginning years of ministry. One question that this phenomenon poses is why God would allow a misplacement in calling to occur or allow an uncalled pastor to continue to lead His bride for many years, only to remove them through this phenomenon much later in ministry. Six of the cases happened after twenty-five-plus years in ministry. In the category of 0-to-5 years, one can assume a portion of those could be related to having a pastor who was not really called to this ministry position, but it would seem that this would decrease the further one progresses in ministry years. Out of all the individuals contacted for interview, I found only two who found alternative ministry positions other than the pastorate and who felt as if the second type of ministry better fit their callings. Most declared that although the phenomenon took place in their ministries, it did not change or alter their calling, and this was true even for some who are no longer in ministry.

One must not overlook the fact that 30 percent of the events took place within the first five years of ministry, yet when looking into the actual stories, which will be done later in this chapter, and when looking at the so-called rookie mistakes made by the pastors, it can be determined that none should have been fatal flaws or should have been treated as such. The pastors who experienced the event much later in ministry also relayed no such flaw issues with other churches in their ministry and one wounded pastor served in his church for almost twenty years before a "fatal flaw" emerged. Had this just been hidden or tolerated or is something pointing to a different cause. The chart proves that this phenomenon can happen at any point in pastoral ministry, which may indicate that there is a flaw in the church resulting in unjustified terminations and resignations. The data indicates that no amount of ministry experience will keep this phenomenon from occurring, nor is ministry experience necessarily preparing the pastor to deal with the causes and effects of this phenomenon. This is the very reason that a strategy was developed to heal from the hurt and pain that this causes.

Question Five: What was the approximate size of the congregation where the event took place?

The fifth chart, Size of Congregation (Figure 5), like the other categories, indicates that the phenomenon of unjustified termination and resignation is not limited to any certain size congregation. The

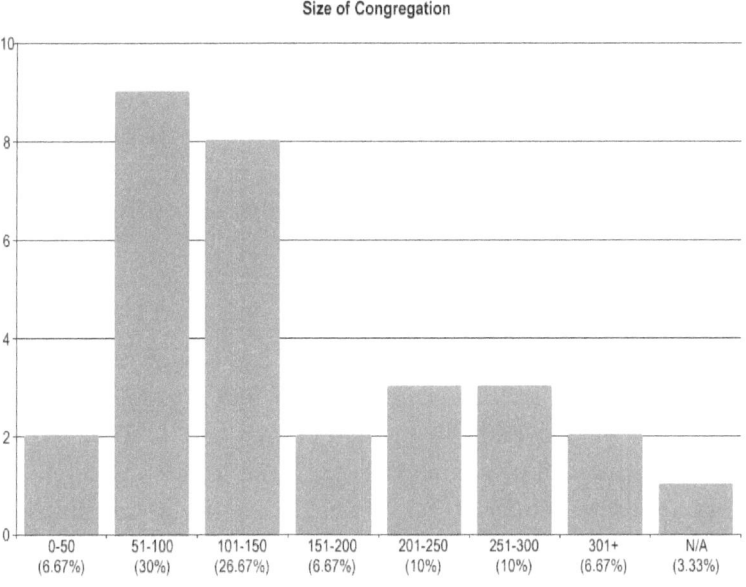

Figure 5

instances interviewed were found fairly evenly throughout all church congregational sizes and locations, with one-third of the events taking place in churches of over 150, which most persons would assume would have multiple staff positions and a very different leadership structure and dynamic than that of smaller, single-staff churches. There were only two events in churches of less than fifty, and it is unknown as to why this is the case, although many churches in this category may have bi-vocational pastors, enabling the pastor to lead through the issues that often contribute to the phenomenon in a very different manner. The reason for this is the fact that finances tend to play a large role in the event. Churches often use the issue of salary as a weapon to their advantage, with several wounded pastors reporting that the churches withheld pay or used the promise of a severance to move the pastor toward resignation.

The interesting piece of information, as seen in the chart referenced above, is the number of cases that are found in the 50-to-150 congregational size category. These results initially led me to determine that this was a more prevalent problem in this category as compared to all other categories of church size. There is something to be said about issues that arise in single-staff churches or churches where there is only one vocational pastoral position and all others are volunteer, in that it lends itself to many of the leadership problems and causations that result in this phenomenon. There is a higher probability in single-staff churches for others to elevate themselves to improper leadership levels and understandings, especially when there is a pastoral vacancy or greater pastoral turnover. Still, one must be careful in not allowing the data to cause tunnel vision when dealing with only this size category. For example, most churches in the Southern Baptist Convention fit into this category.

In a 2017 article written by William Thornton, "The Strange World of SBC 'Small' Churches," Thornton refers to the 2015 Annual Church Profiles and states that the average size of all churches reporting in that year was 145 members and the median church had 70 members.[20] The reality is that the majority of churches in America are in the 50-to-150 category and one should naturally garner more results in this category because there are simply more churches of that size. However, when one gives equal weight to the occurrences of the phenomenon related to the number of churches in each statistical category, one can actually determine that the issue of unjust termination and forced resignation is happening at a much closer percentage in each category than is revealed by this chart alone. The analysis of this data reveals that a pastor may find himself unjustifiably terminated or forced to resign regardless of church size or location.

Question Six: Did you spend any time away from ministry after the event and if so, how much?

The sixth chart, Time Away from Ministry (Figures 6 and 7), ultimately provided me with more questions than answers. The data revealed almost equal numbers between those who spent no quantifiable time away from ministry (eight subjects) and those who spent a year or more away from vocational ministry (eleven subjects) with no real understanding as to why each group can be equally successful in vocational ministry reentry. There was also no data that fit a category of six months to one year, which seems to indicate that if the individual spent greater than six

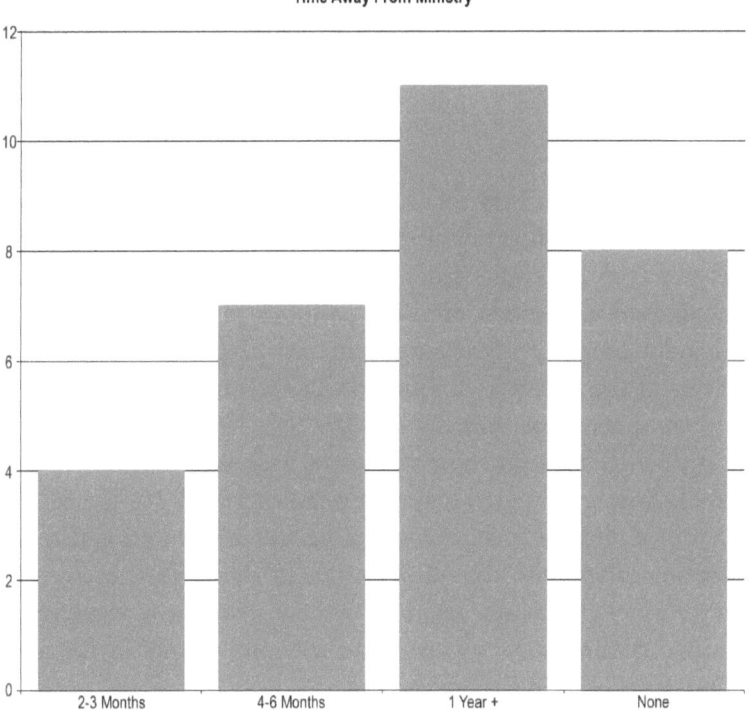

Figure 6

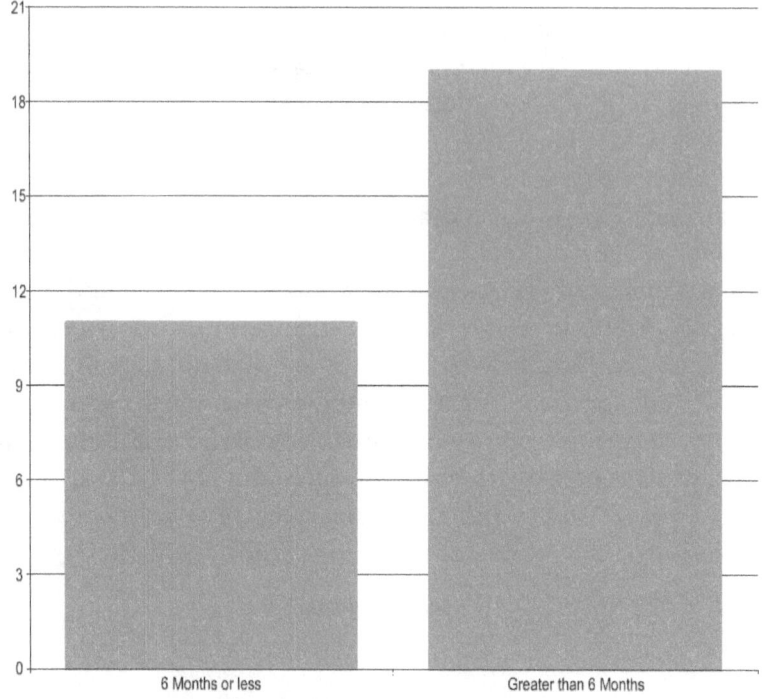

Figure 7

months away from ministry they did not go back until at least a year had passed. However, nothing revealed why this is so. The individuals studied who relayed multiple events tended to show a pattern of longer times in the interim period between ministry positions as each event took place, but it cannot be proven that longer interim periods played any role in the success of the ministers in question in their current positions. Most the subjects spent more than six months away from ministry when the data was divided between those who went back into ministry within six months or those who waited longer at a ratio of 19-to-11. The interviews also identified three who have not yet returned to vocational ministry. This does not align with the 60–70% rate of those who never return to ministry. At first glance, this seems to be a failure of the research to match an expected finding; however, many of the interviewees in the network would not have been in that category.

I found it difficult to identify very many who were not in vocational ministry, possibly because they no longer connect with pastoral networks and are much harder to identify. Therefore, there is great hesitancy in reading too much information into this data. The idea that may be shown in the next section of analysis is that there is no magical time frame for a healthy interim period; however, a strategy must be worked through to be successful. It may be said that different people would work through the strategy at different paces and the severity of the event would also play a role in determining how long the healing process should be. The only conclusion that can be drawn is that enough time should be taken to heal before reentry into vocational ministry is undertaken and that differs for each person.

The remaining question for further study is whether a longer time away from vocational ministry would contribute to healing and allow for a more successful return; one would assume the answer would be yes. Furthermore, there was no category or study conducted that revealed where individuals are in their current vocational ministry positions and whether they would deem those positions to be safer or even successful. Does taking more time away from ministry provide for a more successful return to ministry? At this point the answer would probably be yes, providing a strategy could be followed for healing that included economic stability as the first step. Taking into account my personal experience, as well as some of the experiences from the stories of those interviewed, I have realized that several of the subjects returned to ministry too quickly, perhaps due to economic constraints.

Question Eight: Did you receive a severance package after the event and if so, how much in terms of months or weeks of salary?

The next category of data dealt with the issue of severance (Figures 9 and 10). The information provided by interviewees was largely expected yet shows some interesting analysis. Surprisingly, most of the pastors interviewed received some severance, but they fell into the category of forced resignation. As previously discussed, this was because, after much force was applied, the pastor felt that resignation was the only option available and there would be some negotiating room left if resignation was chosen. The study did show that those who were unjustifiably terminated did not receive any severance at all, which may explain why many pastors facing this problem simply choose to wave the white flag and resign while obtaining whatever severance they can. Economic factors led their decision-making process.

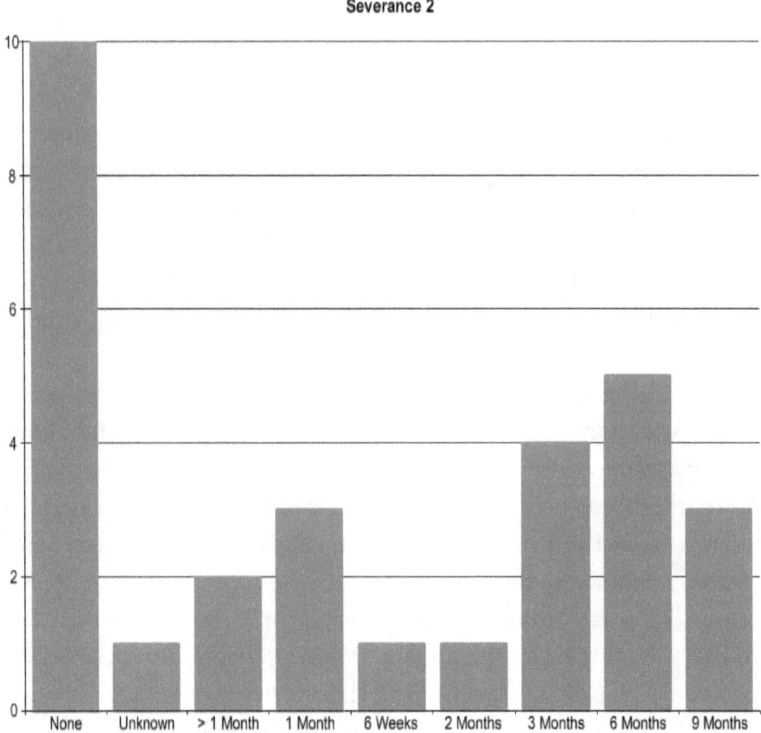

Figure 9

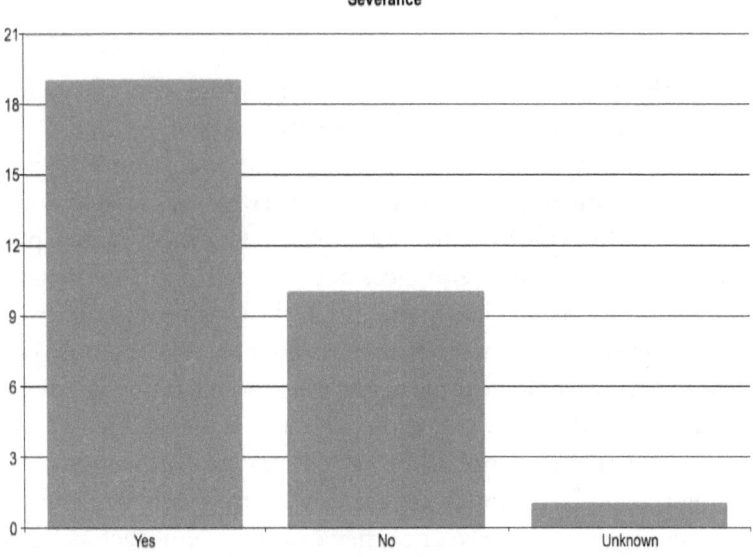

Figure 10

The other factor shown in the severance data was that most did not receive enough severance or pay to last through the average ministerial search process, which is about six months. The lack of severance exacerbated the situation and may explain why many pastors never move very far in the healing process. The pastors are forced to remain in survival mode just to pay the bills instead of being able to heal. This lends credence to the issue surrounding some of the ministries that exist to help pastors through this process. Even if pastors wanted to take advantage of these healing programs, the lack of severance and economic stability keeps these and other resources out of reach.

There are no real guidelines or understandings as to how much severance is needed or is proper when a pastor abdicates his position for whatever reason, especially when most of the fault lies with the church. Churches may set whatever they deem appropriate as severance and, as the data shows, usually the amount falls woefully short of the assistance needed. The subject of appropriate severance would be a very good area for future study. The need exists to develop a better guide to the severance process, although with the autonomy of the local church, there is no real burden for the churches to adopt it. Often, the economic factor is used as a way of punishing the pastor who is being forced out, and this can be a very sinful process, as seen in personal experience and through the stories of pastors. I have seen cases (not in any formal study) in which churches provided more care and a benevolent severance to a pastor experiencing a justified termination/resignation due to a moral or ethical failure than one subjected to an unjustified termination/forced resignation. Are churches taking better care of blatantly sinful pastors than those who are unjustifiably terminated? In many cases the answer to this question is an unfortunate yes.

Question Nine: Did you have a mentor or another pastor that guided you through the process of the event, and if so, was this person inside the church or outside the church where the event occurred?

The last section, the issue of mentor (Figure 11), shows that a slight majority, 56.6%, had help through the process from someone they trusted, and in most cases, that the mentor was outside of the church for many obvious reasons. At this juncture in the research, it is unknown as to whether having a mentor played a vital role in successful ministry reentry. The participants in the study who never reentered ministry were equally divided as to whether a mentor was useful, so the importance of a mentor is inconclusive. In my personal experience, mentors provided invaluable resources and wisdom, which paved the way for successful reentry into ministry. Mentors may simply not know how to lead the pastors, again indicating the need for a strategy; however, mentors are still vital to the strategy. This reveals another area for future study—developing a guide for mentors to help lead pastors through unjustified terminations and forced resignations. I have included a chapter, written especially for mentors and coaches, to see the review of a few available resources that they may find helpful in helping pastors navigate these troubled waters.

The difficulty and frustration in dealing with data collected to this point is that one cannot simply point to a single category to effect change that would prevent this phenomenon from happening. The phenomenon of unjustified termination or forced resignation is no respecter of age, size of church, education, years of ministry experience, or even location. This seems to indicate that, although pastors are not perfect, such terminations are unjustified and the issue is a heart issue lying at the congregational level.

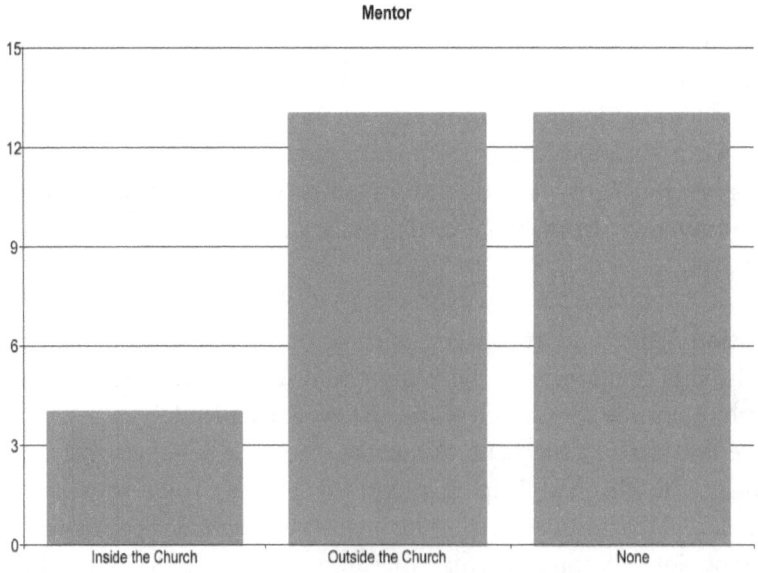

Figure 11

Final Thoughts on the Data

There were not many other projects or much research to guide the expectations of this study and no real playbook as to how to go about gathering the interviews of the subjects being studied. However, with that in mind, there were a few things that happened during this study that were unexpected.

The first unforeseen cause within the project was the time frame which it took to gather the interviews. I had laid some groundwork prior to the project phase, and while researching and writing the previous chapters was able to develop a known network of pastors and church leaders who had experienced the phenomenon in question. It was assumed that this beginning network would soon branch out and create enough of a base of subjects that the interviews would be easily attained. The other factor that led to this false assumption is that the numbers of pastors and church leaders who had fallen victim to the phenomenon being studied would also lend itself to finding enough subjects willing to share their stories. [21] In fact, once the project was put into place, the gathering of the interviews proved to be far more difficult than I imagined or planned it to be. There was most definitely some naivete on the part of myself, assuming that there would be plenty of subjects to find and choose from and that all of them would be willing to share their stories.

The return rate concerning the initial contact of the pastor and the agreement to participate versus the actual return of an interview proved to be at approximately fifty percent. The written interview guides and materials were only sent to subjects who had verbally or in written form agreed to participate and return the interview. All participants received equal follow-up and contact and one can only guess as to what caused the drop rate of half of the participants. I projected the project to only take one month to receive and process all the interviews. In actuality, it took three months. The delay caused me to consider lessening the goal of the project in order to proceed with the analysis.

The second cause is similar in nature to the first. The majority, if not all pastors, when contacted as to their willingness to share their story and data with me readily agreed and welcomed the guiding documents. Four of the participants who initially agreed to sharing their story, prior to writing the story down, contacted me and informed me of their change of heart and mind. These four simply could not nor had any desire to write down or revisit the painful memories of this event and backed out of the project completely. Two of them had never gone back into the pastoral ministry field, opting to move to military chaplaincy. However, the others had successful reentered the pastoral ministry field, realized the stated goal of the strategy being developed, and stated that their new ministry field is healthy and, therefore, did not wish to bring up the past. I used several means of communication to ensure that all data would be completely anonymous to no avail. I then chose, at this time, not to pressure these individuals or follow up in any form.

Unforeseen Effects

The nature of the phenomenological method understands and accepts the bias that the researcher has experienced the phenomenon being studied and therefore I had some idea as to what the interviews would provide to the research. That is not to say that there were some results and effects that were not unforeseen.

During the initial reading and analysis, I noticed that several of the subjects interviewed had, in fact, experienced several events within the scope of their ministry experience. This would constitute a separate individual instance due to the fact that although the minister was the same, the location, the church, and the people involved had changed. This is also true of my experience of the phenomenon and will be dealt with further in the next chapter and analysis of the project. The quantitative data collected also led the director to deem it necessary to treat each individual "event" or incidence as separate and on equal footing in order for the data and resulting charts to be accurate and viable. I then relisted the data creating a list as each individual "event" recorded, due to the change of location and people involved, which brought the total events interviewed to thirty, meeting the initial goal set prior to project launch.

The second unforeseen effect involved the actual filling out of the written guides by the subjects being interviewed. Simply put, not every pastor or church leader filled out the interview equally and with as much information. The responses ranged from just answering the specific questions with little or no explanation, to just writing a narrative of the story with no mention of the directive questions, to just sending in the quantitative data. The written guide was written specifically enough to garner the responses but loosely enough to allow the participants some freedom in writing. The pastor's confidentiality was protected because they included only the parts of the story that they deemed necessary, fitting the confines of consent to use the information.

The last unforeseen effect was the building of friendships and bonds with those who have traveled a path similar to the one this project director has traveled. Communication has continued with several of the individuals who submitted stories and has provided times of counseling and prayer for both the fellow wounded pastor and myself.

I do not believe that these unforeseen effects and events altered the results of the study but proved to be very educational in my own practice and the development of the end strategy that is seen in this very book you are now reading.

I want to now spend a few minutes looking back briefly to where we have been thus far in this book. A sort of internal evaluation before moving on to the stories and the strategy. Let us look to where we have been before we move on the goal of the journey, a strategy of healing for the wounded pastor.

Ministry Setting Evaluation

With the progression of the project through each stage, I have realized how new this topic is to scholarship and even to discussion among pastors. A mentor of mine recently described the project as a Lewis and Clark project in that we know this land exists and many have discussed what may lie within its boundaries, but very few have taken on the task of discovery.

Very careful attention was paid to defining terms in the first chapter, with little knowledge of this project's final form. Boundaries had to be defined before any subsequent exploration could be done. Upon reading the ministry setting, it was determined that extra time in carefully defining the phenomenon was necessary and helpful to set the stage for this project. In short, the ministry setting took on the task of identifying something that everyone knew existed, but few had defined. The equivalent would be attempting to draw the map of a place one wished to explore before setting out on the trip, with little understanding of the landscape.

Another issue for further evaluation is the prevailing question that was asked and answered in the first chapter. This question dealt with the ability of the pastors interviewed to look beyond the pain of the incident and tell their stories as objectively as possible while providing enough information to elicit a complete view of the problem, leading to a strategy. This will be better unpacked in the evaluation of the stories themselves;

however, it may have been naïve to think that everyone who submitted their stories would not be reticent in providing certain details. In Chapter 1, the answer to the prevailing question was yes, that everyone would be too open and self-evaluating, demonstrating the ability to "get the log out of their own eye." Most of the pastors interviewed were able to freely share their stories while being appropriately introspective concerning their faults and shortcomings while some never arrived at this point, which reveals the scope of the problem and the need for a strategy. Several of the pastors interviewed and some who refused to be interviewed have not made much progress in healing and they remain broken pastors or are out of the ministry.

The hypothetical presupposition also proved to be challenging. The goal was for a fully developed strategy to emerge through the telling of the stories. The question is whether this was accomplished. The answer is partially. The evaluation of the interviews will show what strategy has emerged; however, to call the strategy complete may be ambitious. This is not considered a failure of the project because this project ventured into an uncharted forest and deposited some building blocks useful for future exploration. If asked whether this project accomplishes the mission stated in the first chapter, the answer is yes and no. Evaluation of the data and interviews indicates the strategy is far from complete, but enough was revealed to begin the healing process for the pastors, understanding more must be done to finish the exploration of this phenomenon.

Evaluating the Data

I do not wish to spend much time here due to the fact that each chart was presented with an explanation of the information it contained. I will, however, mention the fact that the select few that have seen the data before the writing of the book all were surprised at the findings. This is truly a phenomenon that is no respecter of position, location, church size, timing, or educational level. The data proves finally that this phenomenon can no longer be ignores but must be faced head on and dealt with in order for churches and pastors to begin to find health and growth.

Conclusion

As previously noted, this project is walking into uncharted territory. The benefit of this is that where little is known, every piece of information or story told adds immense value to the study. The slightest bit of a discovery adds great value because the pool of information is relatively small. The difficulty of discerning how to proceed is unknown and unsure because there is little practice to build on from scholarship and study in the past. The next chapter will take a look at the Biblical examples of the four quadrants of termination, detailed in Chapter 1, to give an example of each type of termination. I will spend a greater amount of time in the life of David as an example of unjustified termination and forced resignation.

"This took me almost three years to overcome. I had told myself that I would never preach, pastor, or participate in ministry again."

—*A Wounded Pastor*

chapter five
BIBLICAL EXAMPLES—PART I
Justified Termination, No Termination, Mutual Termination

Introduction

The goal of the Biblical example is to look at the many characters contained in God's Word to discern any similarities in their stories with the phenomenon described in Chapter 1. I found within the progression from prophet to king, as found in 1st and 2nd Samuel, a succession of characters that fit each one of the categories previously in this work. The challenge is that the structure of the church and the pastorate is far different from that of prophet and king in the Old Testament culture; however, these men were in positions of leadership and the group of people that they were entrusted to lead was God's chosen nation Israel. Therefore, correlations can be made between their positions and the position of the pastorate.

I understand that some differences in culture and time apply to these examples and admit that there is not a one-to-one correlation between prophet and king with the lives of pastors today. However, with these differences understood, the lessons remain true.

In order to use the Biblical examples as they fit the phenomenon, there are three main concessions that must be made. The first is the glaring difference in the polity of the congregation or people. The prophet and/or king role was appointed by God with no real choice made by the people, other than their demanding a king so that they could be like the other nations around them, which was viewed as disobedience to God. The pastor role is also appointed by God, to which every church admits, yet this appointment is usually done through congregational polity. Dr. Benjamin Merkle, professor of New Testament and Greek at Southeastern Seminary, states, "the authority of pastors is derived: it comes from God (not the congregation). Although the congregation affirms their calling and authority, it's an authority with divine origin. Paul tells the Ephesian elders the Holy Spirit made them overseers (Acts 20:28) and later indicates leaders are gifts given by Jesus to the church (Eph. 4:11)."[22]

The second concession is that in the Old Testament, as in a monarchial system of government, the king largely exercises abstract authority. The pastor, in today's church polity, must work closely with the people and in fact in some cases the "true" and acting authority in the church lies with the people. When looking at the stories found in Scripture, whether they enjoyed abstract authority or not, the decisions that the leaders made either positively or negatively impacted their tenure of leadership. The lessons that were learned from their leadership can be applied to the pastoral role of today.

The third concession that must be addressed is that the church of today is vastly different than the nation of Israel or the New Testament church. One cannot simply consider the Scripture to find the pastoral role as it exists today. This truth is not a negative or a positive but merely a product of time and change. The culture is different, the people are different, and the polity is different, yet this still does not take away from the lessons learned and comparisons that will be made. In this section, I will attempt to look at these stories and make careful comparisons, asking if these men had been pastors how their lessons and choices would have been applied.

The Biblical example chapters will be structured in a manner to outline a Biblical character that fits within each of the four quadrants of the "Justified vs Unjustified Pastoral Termination/Resignation" chart found in Chapter 1. The Biblical characters in each quadrant will be briefly discussed with evidence showing why they fit into their assigned category. This chapter will detail the first three quadrants and their Biblical character counterpart in order to give context to the issue as a whole, and the next chapter will take an even deeper look through the eyes of David at the experience of unjustified termination/resignation. This will be dealt with as if the character has been interviewed as a part of the project, and the four main categories of emphasis that will be analyzed will include emotional, spiritual, economic, and leadership lessons and strategies that were—or possibly could have been—applied. Completing the Biblical examples will be a New Testament example detailing the phenomenon of the antagonists within the church and how they should be dealt with, detailing one of the main problems that has led to this phenomenon in churches.

Justified Termination/Resignation: The Prophet Eli

The first time the prophet Eli is mentioned in Scripture (1 Samuel 1), it paints for the reader a picture that is seemingly quite normal. Eli is the prophet and high priest of Israel, and his two sons Hophni and Phineas were priests in the temple. The interchange between Eli and Hannah, who was quite distressed at the fact she was barren, gives us a picture of a prophet who was fulfilling the duties given to him by God. Eli's prophecy concerning Samuel's birth was shown to be truthful in the very next verse written.[23] This speaks to the calling and validity of the prophet and his position. The reason that this prophecy is important is that it shows that Eli was truly called and placed in this position by God to lead the people. The mistakes and falling away that would soon be shown do not take away from the fact that the calling and position were sure, and God ordained.

1 Samuel 2:12 begins the falling away of this prophet of God. The question that must be asked is "What caused this prophet to fall away and thus justified his removal from the current position of leadership?" The problem started with his sons, Hophni and Phineas; 1 Samuel 2:22 shows the reader that Eli was older now and had a viable ministry to this point, when it was found that "his sons had been laying with the women who served at the doorway of the tent of meeting." Eli attempted to deal with the situation in going to his sons with a strong rebuke stating that no one would be able to intercede for them if the Lord rebuked them. Eli should have done more here! What is not seen is the removal of his sons for this blatant sin. The rebuke seems to fall short due to no action taken having been by Eli as the prophet and leader. Six verses later, Eli received his own rebuke.

The text begs the question, "did Eli not deal properly with his sons because in his heart there was sin going on as well?" The prophet Eli himself had strayed from his duties and the purity that his position required. The bearer of this rebuke to Eli is only known as a man of God; however, the rebuke is not less powerful. Eli's sin was twofold: he was first "scorning" the sacrifice to the Lord, and second, he did not rebuke his sons strongly enough. (1 Samuel 2:29)

The justified termination came in the form of a strong rebuke from God Himself to the prophet Eli, even though it was not realized until later. Eli was allowed by God to continue for a brief period; however, it was his sin that eventually took his life. When the Ark of the Covenant was stolen, and Eli received the news of his sons' death and defeat at the hand of the Philistines, Eli fell back in the wagon in which he was riding and died. The legacy of Eli was that no male of his household would ever serve again in a position that was handed down to the sons from the father. God raised up a better priest and Eli's family was relegated to begging from the temple for bread. They now had to beg for the very substance that Eli had fattened himself and his family.

Eli was a prophet who erred both morally and ethically. The termination, although in a different manner than pastors would experience today, was a delayed event, which was still very much justified, and the termination of Eli was realized in fact by the ending of Eli's life. The point can be made that the delay may have been an exercise of God's grace and mercy and an opportunity for repentance and redemption. Eli did have to endure much grief at the failure and the evil actions of his sons. At one point even his eyesight failed, and he lost the ability to correctly lead the people. God rendered Eli quite ineffective, which also left the people vulnerable to attack from the enemy, specifically the Philistines.

The question can be asked as to whether Eli could have been redeemed had there been true repentance involved and whether this case could have ended differently. In the case of Eli and the justified termination of pastors in today's culture, a clear Biblical mandate had been broken, and the removal of the leader in the position may be necessary to protect the church. Perhaps it may have been possible for a restorative path for the errant high priest to be found, but God believed it was necessary to protect the reputation of the priesthood and the tabernacle by terminating Eli's service as high priest. The reputation of the office of the pastor and the reputation of a local church body today may also make necessary the removal of a pastor from office by a local church body, but such removal must be merited.

Mutual Termination: King Saul

The people of God had been guilty of disobedience and sin leading up to the account in which Saul entered the picture of leadership. A quick overview of a few chapters of 1 Samuel and other historical writings proves that the people had rejected God as their King and the prophet as the representative and demanded an earthly king as was seen in the kingdoms around them. (1 Samuel 8) God told Samuel to honor the peoples' ungodly request and anoint an earthly king to which Saul then entered the picture very much looking the part. The description of Saul in 1 Samuel 9:2 is the very picture one would have in mind when thinking of an ideal figurehead of a nation who could go to battle before them and bring them pride as a people, describing Saul as a "choice and handsome man" and there was "no one more handsome than he." Saul also possessed the perfect pedigree of a king coming from the tribe of Benjamin with his father being a man of valor. Unfortunately, what he possessed in looks, charisma, and pedigree, Saul apparently lacked in character and necessary skills of leadership, yet this was the choice of the Lord.

Diving into the life of Saul and his leadership as the king of Israel would lead one to believe that Saul was most likely lost or at best not following the Lord's direction at all. Before being chosen as king, Saul was sent on a journey looking for his father's lost donkeys, and when success was fleeting, he turned to paying the man of God for information regarding the location. The man of God was nothing more than a means to an end to rid himself of this assignment Saul had found himself undertaking. However, Saul was God's choice for the first king of Israel.

Saul's mistakes as a leader were many, and several are written down for us as examples. For instance, 1 Samuel 14:24 details for us an order that Saul gave to the men serving under his leadership that they were to not eat until revenge was enacted on his enemies. In 1 Samuel 15 Saul disobeys a direct promise from God in which God would punish Amalek, taking matters into his own hands going to battle. This earned Saul a direct rebuke from the prophet Samuel.

This is a case where you have God's people being disobedient and being given a leader that they deserved in that moment, which I believe is something that God continues to do in His church today. There are times when God gives the church the leader they deserve or need in an act of judgment against disobedience by the people. The dynamic between Saul and the people caused a caustic relationship in which both the people and the leader were living in disobedience to God and breaking Biblical commands and structure. King Saul was eventually removed from leadership, as seen in the fact that his sons would never sit on the throne after him and the kingship would be given to a shepherd boy named David. However, it took several years for the new king to be seated on the throne, and Saul spent the remaining years of his leadership neglecting the people of Israel at the expense of going after David's life.

This was again a case of sin on the part of the people as well as sin on the part of the leader and the caustic relationship that it caused. There is much that can be said concerning the reasons why such leadership was allowed to remain for as long as it did or even why Saul was placed in leadership at all. However, in this case, as stated in Chapter 1, the relationship is better broken to which restoration is not needed. The best outcome from such a leadership event is that the leader and the people are both repentant and paradigms change on the part of both parties. The vehicle in which this can be realized exists only if the parties separate and end the caustic relationship so that they can seek the Lord properly.

No Termination: Samuel the Prophet

Samuel enters the story of Scripture "ministering to the Lord" from a young age under the prophet Eli. This was a time in a time that was described as the word from the Lord was rare and visions were infrequent. The reasons behind this are further proof of the claims made above about the prophet Eli in that it is hard to hear from the Lord as a leader when there is sin in the leader's life and practice. Samuel's story shows us servant leadership under difficult circumstances, yet even with these circumstances, Samuel grew in knowledge and stature with the Lord.

Samuel's call came on the heels of the predicted removal of Eli's sons Hophni and Phineas. (1 Samuel 2:33-34 NASB) The very next verse stated God's call of Samuel in which a prophet would be raised up who would be faithful and would do according to what was in God's heart and soul. The Lord even predicted that this would be a position that would not see or need resignation or terminations when it was stated that He would build this prophet an enduring house. The word used here as "enduring" is the Hebrew word *aman*, which carries the meaning of enduring, faithful, established, and sure.[24] The Lord knew that Samuel would be trusting and faithful even under difficult circumstances such as the people calling for a king, which, in a sense, demoted Samuel. 1 Samuel 3:19 is the descriptive verse of Samuel's ministry and calling when it states, "Samuel grew, and the Lord was with him and let none of His words fail." (NASB) There is not much more that I can add to the no termination category and its example. Scripture simply records a faithful prophet, although not perfect, as seen with his sons as well, who served faithfully and enjoyed a tenure free from removal. Pastors would do well to study Samuel's faithfulness as a model of ministry and leadership.

The Biblical study of the first three quadrants; no termination, mutual termination, and justified termination give us context that will serve to uplift the understanding of the final quadrant, which is unjustified termination or forced resignation. Although much can be learned about the pastorate and the church through these characters as they fit the quadrants model, our focus is mainly on the pastors who face unjustified termination. We will turn to that now with the life and practice of David and his flee from the kingdom.

"At first I was angry and felt like the Lord had abandoned me or that I had lost my call to the ministry. I even felt like maybe I had been disqualified from the ministry."
—A Wounded Pastor

"Oh Lord, how my adversaries have increased! Many are rising up against me. Many are saying of my soul, 'There is no deliverance for him in God.' But You O LORD, are a shield about me, My glory, and the One who lifts my head."
—A Psalm of David when he fled from Absalom his son
(Psalm 3:1–3 NASB)

chapter six
BIBLICAL EXAMPLES—PART 2
King David

The story of David is picked up in 2 Samuel 13, in which he was firmly established as the king of Israel and reaping the negative benefits of the promise laid on his household due to his sin with Bathsheba. Amnon, who was in line for the throne, sinned against his half-sister Tamar, which caused Absalom to set in motion a plan to kill Amnon. Incidentally, David was also invited to this event but chose to not attend, which records the first opportunity missed by King David. The reader can surmise that David's presence at this event most likely could have changed the outcome. However, in contrast, some assert that David would have been a target of Absalom as well if he had attended, yet we do not have any evidence that this would have been the case.[25] David's absence at events where he should have been seems to be a pattern, as it was his absence with his soldiers in battle that led to the Bathsheba incident, which shows that no leader is without fault.

David then heard rumors that all of his sons were killed, to which his nephew Joab has to set the record straight that only Amnon had lost his life. Also during this time, Absalom fled the kingdom, which presents the reader with David's second missed opportunity. 2 Samuel 13:19 states clearly, "The heart of King David longed to go out to Absalom; for he was comforted concerning Amnon, since he was dead." (NASB) David, at this point, should have broken the chain of some bad leadership decisions that were also bad parenting decisions. Despite the mistakes made by his son, grave as they were, David should have gone to his son and dealt strongly with his son's actions while showing fatherly love at the same time. Absalom should not have gotten away with the murder of his brother just as surely as Amnon should have been punished for his crimes. David did not act on any of these issues, and this inaction created some of the problems David experiences later in the narrative.

There is some evidence that this verse is better understood, "the spirit of the king was spent for going out against Absalom." This presents a very different picture in that David was not longing for his son's restoration, but that he had spent his energy trying to kill Absalom, and it took three years for David's anger to subside to the point that the ruse of Joab would even be successful in bringing Absalom back into the kingdom.[26] With the two options in play, I believe that the first understanding of this verse fits better with the greater picture given to us in Scripture depicting David's heart. Another problematic question that is presented is why David would pursue so strongly after Absalom and not Amnon when his crime was committed? Whichever way the reader understands this verse, David was at least guilty of some leadership mistakes.

Absalom enlisted the help of Joab to develop a ruse, which worked before in the case of Nathan, in order to be allowed back into the kingdom. The ruse worked, and Absalom was allowed back into the kingdom, but he was not allowed back into the king's presence. Absalom again went to Joab to remedy the situation, but this time he was rejected. This resulted in Joab's field being burned by Absalom, which shows to what lengths Absalom would go to get his way. This was yet another opportunity that was missed by David. His inaction in dealing properly with Absalom allowed the evil in his son to grow. Absalom may have felt relief in being allowed back into the kingdom but resentment at being held away from the king. 1 Samuel 14:33 records the first time in five years that Absalom was allowed to see the king. This was a moment that could have been seen as a crossroads. Would David deal with this son? What action would the king take? David simply kissed Absalom, which is a sign of blessing, but he clearly did not deal with the issues Absalom caused in the last five years. This inaction on David's part may have played a role in Absalom's next move, but at best, David did nothing to prevent it. David again did not handle the necessary issues under his leadership, and he would soon find out that a much greater issue was about to take place.

Absalom, in the narrative of King David's story, played the role that many pastors see in their churches, which is the role of antagonist. Absalom, most likely, did not start out this way and one could even possibly find some redemptive quality in what Absalom was attempting to do in dealing with his sister's rapist. David, however, abdicated his duties, and if he had acted properly, Absalom may have not had opportunity to take matters into his own hands. One cannot say for sure that any action on the part of David would have changed the outcome of this story, but it can be surmised that his complete inaction may have added to the problem.

A leader who is unjustly forced out of his leadership position will always have some culpability, even though it may be minor.

Absalom's usurping of the king's authority was not initially overt. 1 Samuel 15 records for the reader that Absalom simply sat at a prominent position, the city gate, verbally calling the king's authority and leadership into question and stating to all who would hear that he could do much better. Absalom's statement in 2 Samuel 15:4-5, insinuating that he would be a better judge than the king and would hand out better justice, shows how he had begun, at the very least, to desire David's authority as king. At the very least, he was undermining the authority that God had placed in position to lead, a phenomenon that is happening in churches today. David was also most likely unaware that Absalom had begun the slow chipping away at David's position and leadership by simply getting people on his side.

2 Samuel 15:7 informs the reader that Absalom developed another ruse, but this time instead of getting back into the kingdom after an absence, the plan was to take the kingdom for himself. Absalom used something that he must have known would be effective against a king called "a man after God's own heart." (Acts 13:22 ESV) The idea of couching the true and devious plans of an antagonist in the church as something akin to worship or at least the business of the church (seen here in this Biblical account) is something also seen in the church today. The ploy of paying a vow to the Lord was a plan that Absalom would know would be successful. This antagonist had influenced enough people at this time to set his plan in motion, so as he set off under the guise of worship, spies were sent to ready the people for revolt. 2 Samuel 15:12 then informs us as to the scope of the problem. The conspiracy was strong, and the people increased continually for Absalom. David then heard from a messenger that the hearts of the people had been turned toward his son, and David was forced to flee from his own kingdom and position of leadership. David was forced to, in a sense, resign from his kingship due to the antagonistic works of his own son.

Absalom's attempt to remove David from the office of king was unwarranted because he had no rationale given by God for doing so. Drawing from the Scriptural accounts themselves, I believe it was unwarranted to seek David's removal in this way because God did not have another anointed person in the wings to take David's place. Absalom had no Biblical grounds for seeking the removal of God's anointed leader, especially when intending to replace the leader by placing himself in the office, an office for which he was not intended by God, as he was never anointed in preparation for ever assuming the office. Even after David's anointing as the future king during the life and reign of Saul, David would not lift a hand against Saul, knowing that the timing of Saul's removal from office belonged to God alone. Absalom points to no God-ordained rationale for the removal of David from office via a revolt. For the removal of David to have been justified, such removal would have had to be indicated by God and in like fashion, for the removal of a pastor from office to be justified, such removal should be merited, preferably by a Biblical indication of the merit of such an action.

The Four Areas of Strategy, as Seen in the Life of David

Economic Issues

David's exit from Jerusalem is recorded as being "in haste," and one can expect that neither David nor any servants who escaped with him were able to take any supplies for the journey. There is not much recorded for us in this account as to what David or his servants who followed him were able to do to take care of their basic physical needs, such as shelter and food. Scripture does record in chapters 16 and 17 of 2 Samuel two occasions in which individuals or groups not connected to the people of Israel were moved to provide for these needs. The individual in the first account and the group in the second account were either people connected to others that were beneficiaries of David's kindness and compassion earlier in his reign or simply strangers led to assist. In the second case, the help came from those who would, in any other situation, be considered enemies of the people of Israel.

The first account of economic assistance comes from Ziba, the servant of Mephibosheth. Mephibosheth, the disabled son of David's closest friend Jonathon, was given a permanent place in David's household and the promise of care for his entire life. (2 Samuel 4:4–5) The servant was sent with enough to meet the needs of David and his servants for their journey in the desert. Now that David found himself in need, his past help of another was reciprocated in the wilderness. This has also been my own experience and the experience of those who have been interviewed for this study—that, in a time of forced resignation, those that have been ministered to in the past are moved to be able to provide for the needs of the pastor. This help, in David's example, was not, however, without some sting. Ziba stepped out on his own and attempted here to trick David into thinking that Mephibosheth was also attempting to steal the throne.[27] David received economic help, but it seemed to come with the expectations that restoration to the kingdom was not the goal.

The second account of economic assistance that David and his servants received is even more shocking to the reader, as it is seemingly from an unexpected source. This event is recorded in chapter 17 of 2 Samuel when a trio of individuals came to the aid of David and his servants. Those listed are Shobi son of Nahash, Machir of Lo Debar, and Barzillai the Gileadite from Rogelim. It would be easy to overlook the provider of the economic support and look only to the gifts that were brought to "the people that were hungry and weary and thirsty in the wilderness," which are the very things pastors feel in the land of forced resignation and termination. However, the source must not be overlooked. Shobi was the son of a staunch enemy of the people of Israel but, after his father's defeat, was most likely left in charge by David and was possibly loyal to him to some extent. Machir of Lo Debar is one who had given refuge to Mephibosheth and also someone to whom David had shown favor. Barzillai the Gileadite was an older man who obviously had some wealth and who, with no other evidence as to a connection with David, was just a generous benefactor who took care of a man in need and who sustained David and his servants while in the foreign land. Barzillai even rejected any offer from King David to be taken care of upon his return to the throne. (2 Samuel 18 NASB)

The plight of David and his servants while forced from the kingship is not dissimilar to the pastor who is forced to resign or even terminated due to an antagonist such as Absalom being found within the church or any of the other reasons discussed earlier. Those who should have taken care of the antagonists, e.g., the church and the proclaiming believers, are the ones who have rejected the pastor and his leadership. The leaders in this position may or may not have a severance, but in some cases, as with David, they are forced to leave hastily and have no preparations to take with them. These leaders must then look to secular opportunities to find assistance and sometimes rely on the simple benevolence of strangers to get them through this wilderness that they face. It is my experience, substantiated through the interviews of other pastors conducted thus far in the study, that most do not have an economic plan to take care of an event like this, and like King David, they find themselves relying on whatever they can find and the generosity of those who God places in their path.

Emotional Issues

David left his kingdom hastily as a very broken man and it is clear the previous several years of David's leadership have taken a toll on him. 2

Samuel 15:30 shows David in a posture of mourning, walking and weeping barefoot with his head covered, as he went up the mountain and away from Jerusalem. The reader will remember the schemes that came with the economic help from the servant Ziba, the descendant of Saul cursing and throwing stones at David calling his plight "judgment from the Lord" (2 Samuel 16:5–8), and a plot and a threat on his life that had to be thwarted by men loyal to David. (2 Samuel 17:1–4) All of this took place after David was forced out of the kingdom. There is much to be said about the emotional strain from the previous five to ten years of disruption and attack caused by his own son. When David finally was restored to leadership, his restoration transpired with the loss of the very son who had caused the issues in the first place, yet David strongly mourned the loss of this son. To say that leadership cost David a high emotional price would be an understatement.

The reader of this narrative is blessed to have a window into the emotional state and spiritual state, which will be dealt with momentarily, due to a fair number of psalms that were penned by David during his forced removal from leadership as king. A simple and brief overview of a few of the psalms written by David during this time gives the reader a clear view of his emotional state due to being forced out of his leadership position. These emotional outcries that David made show the reader how devastating it can be to lose a position of leadership in this manner. David made statements to the Lord in the Psalms such as the following:

David bemoaned his adversaries, saying, "many are the adversaries that line up against me and they say there is no deliverance." (Psalm 3:1 NASB)

David, in dealing with false accusations, cried out "there is nothing reliable in what they say," yet their words and actions have still caused him to be in this position. (Psalm 5:9 NASB)

David stated that his tears were his food day and night, that his soul was in despair, that he felt rejected by God, and that his heart was in anguish. He was overwhelmed by fear and trembling. (Psalm 43:2 NASB)

The hardest pain that David had to deal with was the fact that all of this was caused by someone so close to him and someone that he had sweet fellowship with formerly. The betrayal of a son was almost more than David could bear.

David finished the emotional lament by stating that his soul had been persecuted and his life was crushed to the ground. (Psalm 42:6 NASB)[28]

The reality of forced resignation or termination from any position of leadership is that it takes a very high toll on the emotional state of the leader, and in order for the leader to be restored to leadership potential, emotional healing must take place. The connection can be made that the economic support that David received may have allowed David to spend some time on his emotional state and take his cries to the Lord in the form of the Psalms referred to above. Emotional healing is vital in that a leader will go back into ministry or leadership handicapped if this healing does not take place.

Spiritual Issues

The first question that must be dealt with in the area of David's spirituality is what makes his situation different than Eli's situation of justified termination. David was, in fact, also guilty of a moral failure in his dealings with Bathsheba, which had led to the very turmoil that was on his household in the first place. The difference is that David repented and was restored, whereas Eli showed no repentance for his failures. David dealt properly with his sin before the Lord (see Psalm 51 and his confession and restoration), and because of this repentance, David was restored to leadership and ministry. David obviously had to walk through the consequences of his sin, but his repentance, forgiveness, and restoration puts David in the category of unjustified termination in this example. David was not perfect, but he still should not have been forced from his position of leadership.

David's pattern of writing the Psalms not only shows us the pouring out of his heart and state but then also shows how quickly he turned to the Lord for spiritual guidance. A very important point in the strategy for healing after an event like this is found in Psalm 145 when David remembered the works of the Lord and what God had done in the past. Remembering that God has worked in the past will lead the pastor to an area of comfort and understanding that God will work in the future. David also remained teachable, as we see in Psalm 145 and many other psalms penned by David in which he cried to the Father to teach him to do His will. Another important step spiritually is that David remained steadfast in allowing God to fight the battles against the enemy and to not take the battle into his own hands. David refused to retaliate physically when stones were thrown at him in the wilderness. David realized that ultimately the battle was the Lord's alone. When David was restored, he even mourned deeply at the death of the one who caused this problem in the first place.

David also shows the reader a very important point in the strategy of healing and restoration. David recorded within the words of these Psalms that he intentionally found time to worship in spite of the place in which he found himself. A phrase that resonates over and over in his cries is that he will find his hope in God alone and in God will salvation be realized.

When a leadership and ministry position is torn from a pastor's hand, much like the incident of David losing his throne, one of the hardest things to do is spiritual work and drawing closer to God. David's experience and his words show us that this is a vital part of the healing strategy.

Leadership Issues

The issues of missed leadership opportunities have been dealt with earlier; therefore, more time will not be spent on them here other than to note that there are clear missteps by David in his ministry. It is left to conjecture as to whether the situation would have been changed had David acted differently. Only after dealing with the economic struggles and the emotional and spiritual healing is the leader able to take an in-depth look at his own leadership. David's example informs us that he did not learn certain leadership lessons in the interim time. After being restored to the leadership position, David continued to be very lenient on some characters who perhaps did not deserve such leniency. For example, Ziba was still given land, despite his scheme against David when he was weak and despite the accusations against each other involving Mephibosheth and Ziba. David took the middle ground and divided the land between them, something that would cause some trouble in David's leadership future.[29]

The reader of David's leadership and ministry can surmise at least two lessons that David could have learned from the forced resignation of his position. The first lesson was that David should have been present in his leadership. Several of the issues that David faced were due to the fact that he was not where he was supposed to be as a leader. David's absence in battle with his men led to the decision with Bathsheba, which led to the turmoil in his household. David also did not attend the event led by Absalom in which Amnon was killed. The second leadership lesson that David should have learned was to deal with problems in leadership as they occurred instead of ignoring them. As stated above, David did not deal properly with Amnon's sin, which led to Absalom enacting revenge. David did not deal with his son Absalom's inquiry about returning to the king's house. David ignored his son, potentially feeding the revolt that materialized against him. David ignored large problems that only became larger.

This is the goal of the strategy as shown in David's life and practice. The pastor needs a strategy to deal with the economic issues that a forced resignation or termination causes and the spiritual and emotional healing from the hurt thus caused, and only then will he be able to take an honest look at his own leadership to make necessary changes. The goal is restoration of some to a leadership position, which is something that David realized, but the restoration must be done in a manner that creates stronger leaders. Of course, restoration to pastoral leadership may or may not occur with the congregation that removed a pastor from his position of leadership, but the final goal of this strategy is a return to viable and healthy ministry and leadership. The restoration of a pastor to leadership when his termination was unwarranted will be quite challenging and may not be accomplished without a strategy for healing and growth before and during the realization of a new ministry setting.

Biblical Rationale Evaluation

Our attempt was to provide a Biblical example of each of the four quadrants explained in Chapter 1 without misrepresenting the original meaning of the passage or character studied. The problem was that the pastoral role at the heart of the study did not have a direct correlation in Scripture. The cultural and positional differences of the pastorate today were carefully dealt with and explained, even as concessions were detailed. However, with concessions applied, the broader application was still sound in my opinion. This was not a one-to-one correlational attempt but a look at the spirit of each category in the four quadrants as they existed in characters identified in Scripture. The intended Biblical rationale goal was carefully stated in the beginning of the chapter, and the project director believes that the goal was met with no hermeneutical boundaries crossed.

The Biblical examples used furnished sufficient proof that there was a problem with the way God's anointed shepherds were dealt with in Scripture, King David being a prime example. This carries over to the pastorate today and the problem with unjustified terminations and forced resignations happening in the body of Christ, which is as destructive to the church today as it was to the kingdom David led. The choice to deal with a character-driven study was made to fit with the phenomenological nature of the project, rather than dealing with direct principles in Scripture. Further study of the topic, along with examining other areas identified yet not written about in this specific study, would warrant a more principle-driven approach.

"Immediately they began to lash out at me, telling me to leave everything alone. Although there had been new families coming, new converts, baptisms, and memberships, anger began to be thrown at the only person that seemed logical, the pastor."

—A Wounded Pastor

chapter seven

A NEW TESTAMENT EXAMPLE
A Brief Note on the Antagonist in the Church

I want to now turn to the Bible again to deal more directly with one of the leading causes of unjustified termination and forced resignation in the church, the antagonist in the church and misplaced leadership and control. It has been my experience that one of the main problems that pastors face today, which subsequently either leads to or facilitates forced resignations or terminations, is the antagonist in the church. Dr. Kenneth Haugk in his book *Antagonists in the Church: How to Identify and Deal with Destructive Conflict* defines the antagonist as "individuals who, on the basis of nonsubstantive evidence, go out of their way to make insatiable demands, usually attacking the person or performance of others. These attacks are selfish in nature, tearing down rather than building up, and are often directed against those in a leadership capacity."[30] Many of the Wounded Pastors I interviewed mentioned the existence of this antagonist within their church that greatly contributed to the problems that led to the termination or resignation.

Let me share a few quotes from the Wounded Pastors themselves to illustrate the point:

> *"After four years, a woman who had been close friends with the previous pastor got upset when I preached through 'wives submit to your husbands.' The deacons, all over 65, had become uncomfortable with all of the changes required to deal with all the new believers and young families. The upset woman was loud, angry, and implacable. The deacons asked me to leave, although they decided 6 months would be a good time so it would be after Vacation Bible School."*
>
> – A Wounded Pastor

> *"Church growth continued but not at the rapid pace as with the previous pastor. In the rapid growth, a significant part of the members were middle to upper income. Due to the fact that the pool was smaller and*

the numbers joining now were from the middle and lower income group the latter group began to gain voting power in this autonomous governed congregation. When this became apparent to the controlling members a quiet coup was formed for the purpose of pressuring me into leaving voluntarily. By way of the Baptist grapevine, I learned that simmering beneath much of the discontent was the leaving of the highly popular pastor and folks were mad at him because he left for a larger church with a higher salary. When I received an anonymous letter threatening my family with physical harm, I took action by making the letter public to the congregation. This was followed by a deacon publicly calling me a liar. At the ensuing deacons meeting I resigned."

– A Wounded Pastor

"My forced resignation came in the regularly scheduled deacons meeting. In that meeting I was hit by an accusation that I was not ministering the way a group of deacons wanted. They asked for a recommendation to the church business meeting that I be removed as the church's pastor. There was a second meeting and the main antagonist was asked to attend. It was a replay of the first meeting. I admitted to some failures and asked for forgiveness and asked if we could not as Christian adults forgive each other and work together and move forward. The response was no, it is either you or us."

– A Wounded Pastor

Third John introduces to us the character Diotrephes and details for the reader the game plan of the antagonist and how it leads to the problem that is the very scope of this project.

John recorded in verse 9 that he had previously written something to the church, but it was rejected by this self-appointed leader Diotrephes. In these three verses, John, through the dealings of Diotrephes, showed the reader how to spot the tactics of one who has usurped the leadership of the church in place of the legitimately called under-shepherd. There are four attributes of Diotrephes brought out in this letter.

First, one of the attributes of the antagonist is that they desire preeminence in the body of Christ. Diotrephes was described as one who "loves to be first among them." (3 John 1:9 NASB) This obviously goes against the teaching of Jesus as to servant leadership, and this desire was undoubtedly a sinful one. The desire to be first only came with the understanding that there would be those who followed them, and if that leadership was challenged, then the antagonist attacked. The sinfulness can be seen in this person's reaction when their leadership is questioned. Milton Dunavant states in his article "Diotrephes: the 1st Century Tyrant:"

> "Those who questioned or objected to his directives were sure to become recipients of his malicious words, being charged with such things as: not keeping unity with the brethren, sowing discord, being independent, being proud, causing division, walking disorderly, being heretical etc."[31] It is interesting to note that these antagonists accused those who refused to follow them of the very things of which they were guilty and unrepentant."

The second lesson seen through Diotrephes is that antagonists do not accept Biblical teaching. 3 John 1:9 simply states that Diotrephes did not accept what the Apostles said. The reason that the instruction of the Apostles or, in today's case, Biblical instruction is rejected is because it is a threat to the kingdom that the antagonists have built for themselves. Remember, it is about their desire to be first and not a desire for true worship of the Savior.

The third lesson learned is that antagonists make unjust accusations against those who teach the truth. One wounded pastor described the process like this:

> *"I resigned my position after three years of bickering, false accusations, and difficulties working with certain deacons in the church. They were having parking lot meetings, calling members at home, trying to rally them in order to dismiss me. Years later, all of the deacons of the church contacted me asking for me to forgive them. They acknowledged that the chairman of the deacons allowed the position get to his head. Since then, the chairman of the deacons left the church, but had already done the damage."*

3 John 1:10 states that Diotrephes was accusing John and the other apostles with wicked words something many wounded pastors can attest too. The antagonists will use whatever means to protect the preeminence they have built up for themselves. That includes false accusations that can range from accusations of heresy to, in my personal experience, accusa-

tions concerning the leader's marriage and family. Paul dealt with this in Romans 3 when he was accused of teaching the heresy that one should do evil so that good may come. For the antagonists, like Diotrephes, it all stems from their lust for control, and in order to keep that control, they maliciously attack and spread rumors against God's appointed leader. This usually results in a wearing down of the leader to the point of resignation, which falls within the definition of forced resignation.

The fourth lesson learned from the antagonists is that, like Diotrephes, they push out those who refuse to follow their lead. 3 John 1:10 shows the reader that anyone who was seen as willing to receive the brethren were "put out" of the church. Simply put, if anyone dared go against the antagonist, they were put out of the church. This is seen in the churches today and especially in the area of forced resignations and terminations. The pastor is expected to fall in line with the "real leader," the Diotrephes of the church. Anyone who does not get in line with the "preeminent one," the one who has usurped the leadership of the church, is subsequently removed or pushed out, and sometimes that is the pastor.

This is not an exhaustive list of all that is causing the pushing out of pastors in the church and causing unjustified forced resignations and terminations. The interviews and the study conducted thus far have found that, in most cases, an antagonist is present within the story and many unjustified resignation or termination situations can point to one such character with misplaced importance and ill-gotten leadership as a catalyst in the downfall of the pastor's position as the leader.

John gives at least a beginning to a remedy for a Diotrephes of the church. Verse 11 tell the reader to not imitate what is evil. People must cease following the antagonists and not allow them to keep their control or power. In many cases, for the church to be healthy, one must stand up to the antagonist before rebuilding can take place. Churches must begin to see church leadership in a more godly way and return to a Biblical approach, or this trend of resignations and terminations will continue.

Conclusion

The goal of the Biblical Example journey was to look through the confines of Scripture to find characters who fit each of the categories of resignations and terminations and allow the pastor to identify with the story. I attempted to help the reader understand and account for the cultural differences in leadership between the character studies and the pastoral plight today but still find comfort in the accounts. The lessons of leadership and the understanding of the scope of the problem that pastors face today is strengthened by seeing these Biblical examples. The greater amount of time was spent dealing with the account of David because his story fits the scope of the strategy that is the purpose of this book. The progression of David's life, albeit in this short span of his leadership, bears a similarity to the path that pastors are walking today when they are unjustly removed from their positions of leadership. It is my hope that seeing the strategy unfold in David's life will help the pastor incorporate these truths into their own practice.

Many pastors today also face their own Diotrephes in their ministry and must learn how to navigate this difficult relationship found in many of today's churches. I personally have found comfort in the Biblical account, knowing that some of the great characters of God's Word faced some of the same problems. The issues that pastors experience in spiritual leadership are not new issues that have arisen simply in a new culture. They are the results of being fallen men in a fallen world; these problems are not new, and a strategy to defeat these problems is greatly needed. The intended goal of this book from the beginning has been to help church leaders return to successful ministry after a forced exit. David's life and ministry, together with the Biblical accounts and details in the remaining chapters of the book, indicate that, with a strategy in place, this may be accomplished.

"I was always taught that you love your pastor—no, he is not perfect, but he is the man of God that God has placed in that ministry. There was no love left in that church."

—A Wounded Pastor

chapter eight
COMMON INDICATORS IN THE CHURCH
Why Are Pastors Leaving?

The first chapter of this project introduced the intention to consider the phenomenological method as the best method of mining the experiences of the pastors to get to the heart of a strategy that could help others who experience unjustified terminations and forced resignations. I stated earlier in this work, "it is my opinion that the best way of reaching the heart of this issue and devising a viable strategy is to hear the stories of the men who are victims of this phenomenon." The previous section, as well as the work as a whole, has shone a light into the heart of the problem, and although not an exhaustive explanation, more is known about what is happening in many churches. Through the telling of the stories of unjustified termination and forced resignation the desire was to have a clearer picture of what this phenomenon looks like, what characteristics it possesses, and how to potentially identify the warning signs that this could be happening in a particular ministry. The research that exists at this point has dealt only with the question of whether the problem exists, with little being done to develop something the pastors can use to heal and progress back into ministry. Attention will now be turned to the stories themselves to discover what more can be learned.

The interviews and stories collected for the current project have identified some common characteristics and indicators found in many of the churches where this phenomenon is happening; undoubtedly, there are more factors in play than this short list. Developing a better understanding of the characteristics and indicators, while proposing ways to change this behavior from the perspective of the church, are topics for further study.

The first indicator seen in the church is intrinsic leadership problems or unbiblical understandings of leadership that lead to wrong or unbiblical leadership structures. Many of the stories identified the fact that after arriving as the shepherd of the local congregation, pastors soon discovered someone else was the true and understood leader of the congregation. The wounded pastors may have held the title of pastor, but the real power or influence of leadership lies with the deacons or, as is often the case in smaller churches, with a single family in the church. This manifested itself in this my experience, as well as the interview subjects' stories about instances of deacons holding meetings apart from the pastor or even without the pastor's knowledge, directly evaluating the pastor's performance instead of leaving that to a more balanced team within the church, or conducting other business without the pastor, e.g., controlling the finances of the church without at least informing the pastor.

Much has been written on Biblical leadership structures for the local church; however, in most cases, like those found within the scope of this phenomenon, the leadership structure was broken, misguided, unbiblical, and needing repair. Pastors are not without fault here. Several of the pastors interviewed stated that, in some cases, the previous pastor left a toxic leadership paradigm and the church was reacting to this under the new pastor's leadership, or the previous pastor or pastors in succession left in a manner that created a leadership void or caused others within the church to have to assume positions and authority that was neither Biblical nor healthy. Pastors must also learn to leave a position well and not leave leadership voids that lead to unhealthy leadership structures, which eventually lead to unjustified terminations and forced resignations.

The second common characteristic or indicator is the existence of an uncontrolled and unbiblical actor or agent within the church. Most pastors associated with this project identified or spoke of someone in the church with the spirit of a Jezebel who played a key role in the crisis. This is the antagonist in the church much like Diotrephes that John writes about and was the reason for including Chapter 6 in this book. This person can be either male or female and usually has great influence within the church but may not necessarily be the most visible leader in the church. Usually, this person is a "quiet influencer" until crossed, at which point they quickly emerge in the forefront. The issue that causes this person to emerge can be quite simple. In my personal experience, it was the teaching of a specific passage of Scripture and its application with which this person disagreed. This led to many intense meetings and conversations with the individual in question as well as others they involved during the process. A year-and-a-half battle ensued, even after many attempts at reconciliation and a biblical approach to handle the conflict. In reality, had it not been this issue, they would have found something else to be a means to their intended end, control the church or rid themselves of the pastor.

One pastor identified the Jezebel in his church as a "woman who was friends with the previous pastor yet was upset at him for preaching that wives should submit to their husband." A Jezebel usually has great influence and may have held that influence for a long time. Often, they control the "purse strings" of the church and can act as a one-person catalyst, controlling the decision of the church. Many pastors also identified the fact that those who could have changed the situation or possibly stood up to the powerbroker in the church were intimidated by the person or situation and were unwilling to take a stance, even when it was clearly known that confronting the issue or person would be the right and Biblical thing to do.

There are occasions when the uncontrolled actor or agent in the church assumes the form of what some pastors identified as an entrenched crew within the church, possessing the same characteristics of the individual Jezebel. Interestingly, church growth may happen around this group until they lash out and reassert their position in the church. This is usually when the next characteristic or indicator surfaces: the mobbing effect.

S.R. Vessel, in his 2012 dissertation, and Drs. Dallas and Sheila Speight, in their article discussed in previous chapters, were the first to identify the term "mobbing" that takes place as part of this phenomenon.[32] Vensel defines mobbing as "the intentional or prolonged harassment by members of an organization in order to secure the removal of the leadership."[33] This research dealt with defining the issue of mobbing; however, the stories of the pastors paint a more intimate picture of what was taking place, going beyond a mere written definition. This current project serves only to add weight to this indicator and common characteristic, revealing what is happening in our churches.

With the mobbing effect, pastors see petty things become direct accusations, leading to minor mistakes that grew into fatal flaws. One pastor stated, "my offenses were things like taking the order of service out of the bulletin, moving the coat rack, moving the church offices, wanting to know what committees were doing. I was accused of changing the church bylaws that were changed by the committee and voted on by the entire church without dissent. There was no accusation of immoral or unethical actions."

On many occasions the mobbing takes a more direct approach, i.e., threats of physical violence to pastors or family members, direct accusations, or even rumors being spread in the community with the purpose of damaging a pastor's reputation and causing the resignation. Pastors spoke of rumors attacking their marriage, threatening phone calls, and accusations of crimes. Another pastor relayed that the treasurer of the church refused to pay the pastor's salary and others had bonuses and benefits removed quietly. Unfortunately, the scope of this project does not lend itself to answering the phenomenon of the mobbing effect in churches and what should be done about it. This will be left to projects further down the academic road. One pastor, a victim of mobbing, had this to say: "I have an affinity for Christ's understanding experientially of what it means to be falsely accused, tried, and convicted in the kangaroo court of religious bigotry."

The final characteristic or indicator is unrealistic or unwritten expectations on the part of the pastor or the church. Several of the pastors interviewed, when looking back at the interview process, indicated that the pastoral search team had been less than honest with them. The pastors were promised that their leadership would be followed, that the church wanted change and growth (among the many catchphrases that are said to make sure the pastor accepts the church). One pastor stated, "I came to what was presented as a healthy, happy, growing congregation." Once the pastor is finally on the field, then the church reverts to its standard practices and is found to be vastly different than promised. The search process in the church is broken and must be changed; however, the pastors are not without fault here, a fact understood by those interviewed for this project. The pastors, all too often, go into the search process, even accepting the position, without exploring or demanding clear-cut, written, mutually-agreed-upon expectations of ministry and the expected scope of the pastor's leadership. Approaching the search process in this manner may not cause the phenomenon to cease, but when other factors rise, the pastor can refer to the mutually-agreed-upon direction and leadership paradigm for at least some modicum of support. Pastors could change some of the scope of the phenomenon if they simply required more out of the search process. The pastor interview process indicated that the majority who had been through an unjustified termination or forced resignation later approached the pastoral search process more carefully and with written expectations and guidelines.

These characteristics and indicators are not new nor is this the first time they have been identified however they are a part of the bigger story. There is an intrinsic problem in many of our churches that are causing pastors to be wounded. I have deliberately stayed away from offering many direct solutions to these characteristics precisely because the main purpose of the project was to identify a strategy for the pastors to use in healing after the fact. Perhaps in the future a study can be done as to find solutions for these indicators, however pastors must be able to identify these indicators in their church and be ready to navigate the ensuing storms they provide.

Prior Research: Has Anyone Studied These Indicators Before?

Some may be led to ask, "Is this phenomenon really happening?" or "Why is this happening in churches?" I have found little to no research conducted in this area as to the scope of the problem, yet many admit the phenomenon exists. I also wanted to add some weight to the raw data that will be dealt with in the next few chapters and show that the wounded pastor should never feel alone, isolated, or even as if this only is happening to them. This is a tactic the enemy uses to keep wounded pastors from healing and if they see the data they will know that they are truly not alone.

I personally reached out to several denominational and research leaders in the field of pastoral study and found that no qualitative or quantitative data could be found, yet each member stated that the evidence existed in a hearsay or anecdotal sense. Responses to inquiries for data were met with statements such as this from Dr. Houseal in research services for the Nazarene Global Ministry Center: "Your project sounds interesting, but I do not have any data on whether or not a pastor was unjustifiably terminated or forced to resign."[34] Dr. Franklin Dumond, director of congregational ministries for the General Baptist Convention, stated, "As we discussed in our phone conversation this is a difficult area to study since there are very few if any records of churches and pastors who have found themselves in this situation. While anecdotally I can share about some situations, I also know that many of these conflicts are disguised from outside view."[35]

Two other contacts were made with the goal of finding some qualitative data on the scope of this problem, Scot McConnel of Lifeway Research[36] and Sharon Casada,[37] demographics specialist for the General Council of the Assemblies of God. Both sent the Lifeway Pastoral Protection Study and made mention of the unavailability of statistics specific to the field of study within the scope of this book. I want to share those statistics with you now to show you, yet again, what is happening in our churches today and is largely being ignored.

The Lifeway Pastor Protection Research Study produced a qualitative report called "Reasons for Attrition Among Pastors" and, in this study, interviewed approximately 1,500 pastors between December 2014 and January 2015. The findings make the case that most reasons for pastors abdicating their post are anything but moral and ethical failure and frequently involve unjustified terminations and resignations. With no real concrete evidence one can only guess at this point as to the validity of this being the case. Lifeway's findings are as follows:[38] The top reasons the previous pastor from a church left the pastorate are change in calling (37%), conflict in church (27%), family issues (17%), poor fit with the church (13%), moral or ethical issues (13%), burnout (10%), personal finances (8%), illness (5%), lack of preparation for the job (3%), other (16%), not sure (12%). One can see that many of these categories could potentially be unjustified or forced termination issues.

The study goes on to say that more than one in three pastors experienced a significant personal attack at their last church. The reasons for the attacks are as follows: conflict over changes you proposed (38%), conflict with lay leaders (38%), experienced a significant personal attack (34%), conflict with church patriarch or matriarch (31%), conflict over your leadership style (27%), conflict over expectations about the pastor's role (25%), conflict over doctrinal differences 13%, none of these (36%).

The main reason for including these statistics is to share with you, the reader, the only known evidence that I have found for what is taking place in our churches today and to call direct attention to the problem. I mentioned these correspondences to demonstrate that I made an effort to include research and data from the past, in the area of forced termination and resignation, but it is limited in scope and number. The information that has been found in the research conducted thus far has been simply attributing a reason for pastors leaving the post yet with nothing specifically pointing to the justification of the termination or a strategy for healing after the event. Pastors are left with a lot of reasons but no answers.

The claim that I have made in Chapter 1 is that the reasons, other than for a Biblical or ethical mandate being broken, put these events squarely in the intended focus of study for this book. As stated in Chapter 1, David Roach in his article to the Baptist Press, "Pastoral Terminations: Common but often Avoidable," states:

> "The most common causes of forced termination among Southern Baptists are 'control issues,' 'pastor's leadership style' and 'poor people skills on the part of the pastor,' according to the forced terminations report. Among the top 15 causes of forced terminations, only two are related to sin by the pastor—'ethical misconduct' at no. 8 and 'sexual misconduct' at no. 10."[39]

The second source mentioned previously was an article in the *SBC Life* publication,[40] although admittedly not a scientific study, which conducted some research as to the top reasons for unjustified terminations and resignations. Their top five reasons are, in order, control issues, poor people skills on the part of the pastor, a pastor's leadership style being too strong, the church already being in conflict prior to the pastor's arrival, and the pastor's leadership style being too weak. These issues have remained in the top five steadily over the past several years. Issues such as declining attendance and doctrinal issues are usually found in the number six and seven spots. It is only when one comes to the last three spots of frequency of occurrence in churches that one finds ethical or moral misconduct and dishonesty.

As I have mentioned a few times to this point, I have personally experienced the phenomenon of an unjustified resignation/termination that was caused by antagonists within the church and found few resources, little scholarship, and little or no assistance for pastors facing the difficulties that it has caused. This is what has led to the current project at hand and creating the burden that something may be done to at least call attention to the phenomenon of forced resignations and terminations for unjustified reasons and then advance the scholarship in this field of study.

Conclusion

My goal in this brief chapter was to detail for you the reader some of the common characteristics and indicators that this may be happening in your ministry or a church you are involved with. Although not an exhaustive list of what causes this phenomenon to happen in churches it may help you at least survey the landscape of ministry to see potential landmines, or at least help the pastor formulate questions to ask before entering a ministry. The quotes are from the wounded pastors that were interviews as to what was happening, in their own words, in their own ministries, as to why they were forced to leave their post. I remember as a child watching GI Joe and hearing the slogan, "knowing is half the battle." Pastors must be better informed as to the danger zones in ministry and what may lead to being a victim of unjustified termination or forced resignation. I hope one day work can be done to remedy these things and bring health to the churches themselves but at least knowledge of the indicators and characteristics can allow the pastor to be more careful.

"This experience, for the most part, hammered the final nail in my willingness to participate ecclesiologically with the current system. The harmful influence of a local ecclesiology too heavily invested in a total congregational polity is simply too obvious to be ignored."

—A Wounded Pastor

chapter nine

COUNTING THE COST
Building the Four Stages of the Stragegy

I have modeled for the reader the four stages of the strategy that I will explain in Chapters Ten through Thirteen, which are finding economic stability, emotional healing, spiritual healing, and then learn leadership development lessons. But before I could get to the strategy I had to prove what I had seen happening in our churches through personal experience and through the stories of others. I will detail that journey now and then at the end of this chapter show the strategy through the illustration of building levels of a house, with the end goal of being on the balcony enjoying the view.

How Did I Prove What is Happening in Our Churches?

The world of unjustified terminations and forced resignations is a forest mired in pain, hurt feelings, financial damage, bitter spouses, dying churches, and the list goes on. I have personally walked this path, and I understand the difficult journey this can be. As I traveled this path personally, I found no viable or repeatable strategy to exist for aiding reentry into ministry (restoration) for those who have experienced unjustified terminations or forced resignations. The purpose of this chapter is to detail the plan that was undertaken in order to begin to develop a viable strategy highlighting the four areas of concern each pastor faces, including economic recovery, emotional healing, spiritual healing, and leadership development hurdles.

The emotional, physical, and spiritual harm that comes to pastors by wrongful termination is negatively impacting many pastors in ministry today and a how-to plan for restoration needs to be developed. It was stated in the previous chapters that the majority of those who leave ministry in this way do not go back into a vocational ministry in the future, settling for secular employment instead. The strategy developed in the final chapters of the book, took the stories of men who have walked this path, along with my personal experience, and mined them for a strategy that can be used and replicated when others find themselves walking a similar path.

I analyzed and interpreted the interviews and stories of thirty pastors and ministry leaders who were victims of the phenomenon of unjustified forced terminations and resignations, to bring attention to the issue and to begin to determine the viability of creating a strategy to elevate the percentage of those who successfully reenter the ministry setting and hopefully encourage further study in this area. I also analyzed the steps they have taken in the four distinct areas of concern: economic recovery, emotional healing, spiritual healing, and leadership development. I was able to identify the common steps taken by all those who successfully reenter ministry as well as possible missteps from those who do not enter ministry again and extrapolate a strategy that can be implemented by others who have also been unjustifiably terminated or forced to resign.

The goal, as stated earlier, was to elicit thirty interviews or stories of unjustified forced termination or resignation from pastors, either lead or associate, and to be able to mine those stories for some quantitative data and the emergence of a strategy for reentry into ministry. The quantitative data would be for the purpose of showing trends and the scope of the problem and the stories and interviews of the lived experiences would show the beginnings of the strategy in these four key areas: economic recovery, emotional healing, spiritual healing, and leadership development.

The first step, in the process, was to develop a written guide, which was sent to the individuals who agreed to share their story and would lead them to tell their story. (See Appendix A). The purpose of the guide was to make sure that the subject being "interviewed" would include all the necessary components needed for the analysis and the completing of the project. The interview guide first defined for the reader the project director's working definition of unjustified forced termination and resignation to assist the individual with making sure their lived experience fit the scope of the study. The issue of confidentiality was explained very clearly and then the reader was guided to share their story. The subject was given ample freedom in writing the interview as they chose with as minimal leading by myself as possible.

The next and final section of the written interview guide dealt with some quantitative data questions that would, as mentioned above, seek to develop some trends and percentages that would lend credence to the findings and are shown in the next two chapters. In order to develop these findings, ten data-driven questions were asked of the subject and corresponding charts were produced from the provided data.

In full, forty-two individuals indicated initial willingness to participate in the project and received the previously-stated documentation and guides; however, only twenty-five individuals returned the interviews by either written or verbal means. Throughout the project it was also determined that several individuals had experienced multiple events and a determination was made that each individual event would be counted as a separate interview. This ultimately led to the meeting of the goal of thirty separate events of unjustified forced termination or resignation, along with the quantitative data pertaining to each event.

The method of procuring interview subjects was largely achieved through networking, starting with known associations and branching out from there. The analysis of this method will be dealt with in the next chapter as to the success or shortfalls of this method; however, the nature and sensitivity of the phenomenon made it necessary to build trust with interview subjects before they were willing to share their stories. A few of the pastors interviewed were forced into non-disclosure agreements as a condition of their severance and their trust and understanding of confidentiality was paramount in the development of this strategy. Their sacrifice has made this possible.

Another method of gaining interview subjects was through social media platforms, mainly Facebook, by posting an appeal through two groups that this director has ties with. Those two groups were the Baptist Review Facebook group and the MBTS Doctoral Students Facebook group. This resulted in greater than ten of the total contacts with approximately five actual interviews being sent back to the project director.

I followed a process of daily and weekly email contacts, reminders, and follow-up to reach the predetermined goal stated in the previous chapter of thirty interviews. This was accomplished with twenty-five subjects, totaling thirty individual events. Each subject who agreed to write or share their story was also encouraged to share this process with their own network of pastors and church leaders who may have also experienced this phenomenon. As the interviews were obtained, either through verbal or written means, they were printed and filed for analysis once the final goal was met.

Through the three months that were spent networking and finding subjects to interview, it was found that five of the subjects were not comfortable with writing out their stories, due to the painful nature of the experience. The solution to this was for me to interview the subject in person or over the phone and develop a transcript from the verbal interview. Three other subjects, who initially agreed to conduct the written interview, backed out of the commitment due to the sensitive and painful nature of the subject matter, stating that "the issue is in the past, they had put it behind them, and they did not wish to visit the issue any further."

This process of storytelling and the development of the strategy, explained in detail in Appendix A, is called the phenomenological study method and was found to be the best way to get to the heart of the problem in ministry today, especially since, prior to this book, little to no actual data existed. The method of Phenomenological research is defined by Dallas and Sheila Speight as:

> "... the study of phenomena or the notion of experience that is intentionally focused on the lived experiences of individuals, with a subjective view of how individuals experience the phenomenon and an objective view as to what they have in common with other people having experienced the phenomenon."[41]

The authors go on to list the two main components of a phenomenological study as being the participants who have shared the experience or phenomenon being studied and the fact that the researcher must also share the personal experience of the phenomenon that he or she is studying. Even though the researcher has experienced the phenomenon under review, that does not limit the researcher's ability to objectively study the experience. In fact, the experience of the researcher places them in a better position to understand the issue being studied and extrapolate the correct results or understanding.

The challenge for the researcher conducting the phenomenological study is to understand and admit those biases that they bring to the table, being able to look past preconceived notions and ideas related to their own experience as a victim to develop accurate understandings from the experience of others. This has proven to be a challenge to me, for which careful boundaries have been established to combat the issue. This does not, however, diminish the results but remains only as a caution to the researcher.

In short, researchers using the phenomenological study method take the lived experiences of people who have experienced a certain phenomenon, along with the personal experience of the researcher, to study how the stories relate to each other and to mine those experiences for truth, strategy, or other scientific and research data.

How Did I Get the Stories From the Pastors? Indirect Measurements

Due to the nature of the phenomenological study method, the indirect measurements consisted of the subjects detailing their stories. The interview subjects, as stated above, were given a written interview guide that detailed the scope of the project, defined the key terms, and simply asked readers to share their stories. This project director did include, however, eight bullet point statements to help guide the writing process and to ensure the addition of all the pertinent information needed to begin to develop a strategy.

The interview guide also included ten questions for the purpose of determining the scope of the problem related to cause and effect, weak points in the system, potential access points on which to focus strategies, and general information on this phenomenon.

Those bullet points are as follows:
- Tell your story of unjustified forced termination or resignation.
- What did you do to survive financially? (economic component of strategy)
- What actions did you take on your journey to cope with the event and/or heal emotionally?
- How did this event affect or change your relationship with God?
- Have you been able to identify leadership lessons that were learned during this process?
- Are you currently still in ministry? If not, what vocation are you in?
- Is your current ministry similar to the ministry in which the event took place?
- If you are currently in another ministry, detail the path that you took back into ministry.

It was discovered through this process that no two individuals interpreted the written guide equally; however, enough information was shared to allow the researcher to develop some common characteristics, trends, and details pertaining to each component of the strategy.

Building the House: The Structure of the Strategy

The strategy took the form of building a house with the intended goal of reaching the balcony and being able to see the view of greater leadership skills and return to viable ministry. I took each of the interviews and placed the pertinent information from their own stories into each of the four categories. The process began at this point to develop commonalities and the strategy began to emerge, which is the heart of the phenomenological study method, and was modeled for the reader in the life of David.

The strategy can be compared to levels of the house with the intended goal of moving the victim of the phenomenon from the basement level to the balcony on which they can see their way into a new ministry learning some valuable leadership development lessons that will serve them in future ministries. The basement level is the economic area of concern. When one has been unjustifiably terminated or forced to resign, and as in the case of many in the ministry, no assistance is readily available and few receive severance, this causes the individual to not be able to begin the healing process. As stated in previous interviews and sections of this book, moving forward toward healing cannot take place if one is worried about paying the bills and putting food on the table. This can be the darkest hour and the darkest place as these are issues faced immediately after the event takes place. Once the person can find some way to alleviate the financial concerns, the individual can move to the next floor.

The first floor is the emotional healing that must take place. The lived experiences of those who have faced this phenomenon and my personal story will hopefully provide at least the beginning point to heal emotionally in dealing with the hurt, the anger, the lack of trust, the questioning of one's own ability and character, and all the emotional fallout that occurs in this phenomenon. Unless pastors can

LEVEL THREE
Spiritual Healing

Leadership Development
LEVEL FOUR

LEVEL TWO
Emotional Recovery

Economic Recovery
LEVEL ONE

see through the emotional issues that this experience causes, they will have difficulty moving to the next stage, which is repairing their calling and relationship with the Lord.

The second floor is the spiritual level. Much like David's experience in the wilderness when running from Absalom, the victim of this phenomenon must be able to come to terms with what God has led them through. It is on this spiritual level that the pastor can and should be able to rediscover the call to ministry, to see a call to a different ministry, or at the very least to receive some spiritual healing in their personal relationship with the Lord.

The balcony is the goal of the strategy. It is on the balcony that one can enjoy the view which is a viable and healthy return to ministry. The view in this case is the leadership lessons that one must learn in order to not repeat past mistakes and to strengthen their abilities so that when they run into some of the same issues in the next ministry they are better equipped to handle the situation. It is this clarity that will lead them into a new and vibrant ministry instead of being counted among the high percentage of those who leave ministry altogether.

I found that this is a good way to begin to develop the strategy. As stated previously, no formal quantitative data existed on this problem, yet we know that many pastors fall victim to this phenomenon each year. The pastors who were interviewed in Chapter 1 were more than ready to tell their stories in hopes of helping those who must walk this path in the future and this carried through to the majority of the other pastors who have shared their stories as well. These stories provided the strategy and the commonalities and ideas from those who stumbled their way through this journey, myself included, and will pave the way for a much easier way back for future pastors and church leaders.

Assumptions and Limitations

As with any study of this nature, largely anecdotal evidence and based on the story telling of the victims, there are certain assumptions made before starting the journey and certain limitations in the undertaking of the study. The main assumptions are that the pastors who have faced unjustified termination and or resignation would be willing to write their stories and that by using the guide that will be provided, the information will cover all four categories within the strategy. One major concession is that most of the interviews will be from those who have made it back into ministry, which is vital to closing the ministry gap with the strategy. The intended goal has been to not only seek healing for these men but also to diminish the numbers not returning to any form of ministry. I also assumed that a strategy could begin to be developed utilizing commonalities within the stories with the understanding that this is just the beginning look into a very deep and understudied subject.

The first limitation is that the project will be kept only within the confines of Evangelical denominations, with the bulk of the interviews coming from the Southern Baptist denomination. This is primarily because the I have spent the totality of my ministry in the Southern Baptist Convention. However, attempts were made to gather some interviews from other denominations. This did not affect the strategy that emerges because the lessons learned will be assumed to be universal in nature and practice to any denomination. It is also understood that non-Evangelical denominations may experience a form of this phenomenon; however, the polity of each denomination would deem a different approach to building a viable strategy. This phenomenon is more prevalent but not limited to those denominations in which autonomy of the local church is a major factor in the polity and structure.

The second limitation of this project is that the interviews consisted of only male senior and associate pastors who fit the criteria of the unjustified termination or forced resignation category. Those who have been terminated due to ethical or moral reasons simply do not fit the confines of the project.

The final limitation is the understanding that the number of interviews will be rather small compared to the number of cases involving this phenomenon. I understand the personal limitations and time constraints that are implied when the research is a team of one; however, using the phenomenological method may prove that a smaller yield could produce equally trustworthy and valid results. This is only the first foray into this forest, and it is understood that much more is needed in this area; this project director hopes that more will take up this issue in later research.

Conclusion

I know that this is only the beginning and this process will most likely create more questions than answers; however, at the very least, the issue will be raised and brought to the forefront. The conversations had around the coffee shop with other pastors are met with a clear understanding that this must be studied. There may be more than just the four areas of concern that arise from the journey. However, the premise from the beginning has been to start the journey and to begin what the Drs. Speight stated in their own study—that more must be done. Hopefully healing will be brought to some through the tears of others.

The strategy detailed in the following chapters is a four-phase plan that deals with the four main components pastors must walk through to heal from unjustified termination or forced resignation with the goal of successful reentry to ministry. The strategy, as shown in the diagram in a previous chapter of the levels of a house, is meant to be a progressive plan dealing first with the most pressing issue facing the pastor after the event takes place, which is that of simple economics. The strategy then moves to emotional healing, which leads to and is connected to spiritual healing. The final phase of the strategy requires pastors to be able to take an honest and direct look into the heart of their leadership and see what changes must happen or which lessons must be learned so that they may be more successful in their next ministry assignment. The disheartening finding, revealed through writing this book, is that many do not make it to this last level. In fact, some reentered ministry without any quantifiable healing sustainable leadership lessons learned, aside from survival skills and avoiding the problem again at all cost. The inability to progress through all four levels was the cause of not reentering the ministry again or the cause of multiple events of unjustified terminations or forced resignations being experienced by several of the subjects in this study.

The strategy is, unfortunately, in its infancy and is not as complete as I had hoped it would be. Yet, with the understanding that this is such a new field of study, one finds comfort in the fact that something is being developed and hopes that further study will complete what has been considered thus far relating to unjustified terminations and forced resignations.

We will not turn to the first level of the healing strategy which is the struggle with the economic impact a loss of ministry has on a wounded pastor.

"I received a two-month severance package from the church. I have since learned that the average severance package for someone with my tenure would have been six months. It has been four months since everything happened. I am currently working three part time jobs in addition to writing projects and looking for full time work."
—A Wounded Pastor

"When I discovered the fact that it was either resign or be fired, my focus shifted to negotiating my release and getting whatever I could to take care of my family for as long as possible so I could find another ministry position. I was lucky to get a six-month severance, but the time in between ministry positions was over a year."
—A Wounded Pastor

chapter ten
A STRATEGY FOR HEALING— ECONOMICALLY

The first level the pastor must navigate is the economic impact that results when the income of ministry is taken away and the severance is found to be woefully short of that which is needed, and the pastor finds himself in survival mode. I remember the first time this phenomenon happened in my ministry, having a deacon call me and expressly tell me, "just send your resignation letter with me and we will see what we can do." I can assure you that in many of the cases for these pastors walking this journey, financial concerns are not at the heart of those leading the charge against them. In my previous ministry, when it was clear that I would either resign or be fired, I pulled from my previous experience and had written out a detailed list of demands in exchange for resignation. This was also the experience of several of the pastors I interviewed. The economic impact from these events in my own life included extensive debt to survive the interim, two short sales of homes, and at one point moving in with family. In short, the economic impact of this kind of event in a minister's life can be extensive enough to cloud any attempts at healing and moving forward.

The process of healing cannot properly begin because bills must be paid, and a formal system of assistance is not usually found or available. Pastors cannot take advantage of normal secular avenues of financial assistance, and therefore, most find themselves lost as to where to turn. This issue can also delay emotional healing because counseling is quickly ruled out as too expensive or simply unavailable. Many of the pastors interviewed did, however, note miraculous giving from those within the Body of Christ, some even coming from individuals within the church where the event took place. This seemed to help in the emotional category as much or more than in the economic category because the gifts usually fell short of what was needed for long-term stability.

The tactics the interviewed pastors used for financial support seemed to be all over the map. Some pastors developed a "whatever-I-can-find" mentality, taking whatever odd or temporary jobs were available. Most jobs taken immediately after the event took place reflected at least a 50% salary reduction compared to salaries paid by the church. Others took on interim pastorate positions, which could be good or bad depending on the location and potential lack of healing. Some pastors, myself included, were forced to live on credit, something they would never advise a church member to do, and some carry this debt for several years following the event.

The components of a usable economic strategy, sadly, are available largely in the secular world and at this point and must be explored and developed into a structure for pastors to employ.

First, pastors must do a better job of being ready to be tentmakers if the situation requires it. The pastors who developed skills, a profession, or educational proficiencies outside of ministry tended to do better during the financial crisis. It is important for pastors to have a "tentmaking" option as they enter and walk through their ministry career. In one case, the pastor described a scenario in which having education only in ministry areas hindered his gaining secular employment. Pastors must ready themselves for the event when secular employment is desired or, in this case, is thrust upon them, even for a short time. The statistics have proven that most every pastor will indeed rely on some form of secular employment at some time in their ministry.

Secondly, pastors must be willing to take lesser employment. One pastor worked on a road crew and another in the hospitality field at a vacation destination and both, upon reflection, noted that the time in this "lesser field" proved to be a prominent component of the healing process. Stepping away from the rigors of ministry and simply punching a clock and earning a paycheck for a time is not a failure and is a time in which economic burdens can be alleviated. This type of employment is also a time in which the pastor can complete the job without taking it home with them, helping the emotional component also. Some pastors interviewed, upon reflecting on their journeys, found that they faced trepidation or an unwillingness to take on a job for which they were vastly overqualified, extending the economic pain, which caused a few to reenter ministry too quickly and led to an increased potential of the event repeating itself. This also may manifest in an unwillingness to take on a smaller or different ministry position than that of the previous place of ministry.

Pastors must be very careful not to buy into the world's view of success, thinking that bigger is better and that ministry is a ladder to climb. One pastor that I interviewed related to me, after being terminated from a church most pastors dream of pastoring, that he has found peace and joy in pastoring a smaller country church and is even driving a bus for the school district. His words to me were, "I am happier in ministry than I have ever been. I am currently pastoring, at the time of the writing of this book, what would be considered a smaller rural ministry, yet I have found the most genuine, healing group of believers that I have ever pastored. My return to ministry has been successful largely in part of God using this "smaller" ministry in order for me to be healed emotionally and spiritually." The lesson is that pastors must redefine what success looks like and simply be obedient to where God is trying to place you in ministry. You may find healing in places you never expected it to be.

Thirdly, pastors must develop a plan of economic attack in case the event of unjustified termination and forced resignation occurs. The position of the pastorate, or other church leadership positions, must be understood to be in the category of high-risk professions, in that there is a great possibility of pastors finding themselves unemployed or underemployed. This is a category that many pastors remain naïve to and for which they are unwilling to prepare. Pastors and church leaders must understand this possibility and have a plan in place to meet the challenge. No pastor desires such a plan, but if the economic impact is lessened to any degree, then the rest of the strategy may be completed more quickly. I reached out to Robert Mikkelsen[42] of the Cardinal Investment Group to discern a possible plan for any professions at a high risk of turnover or unemployment, and pastors would do well to heed the advice.

The plan for financial stability in the case of a sudden loss of employment stemmed from the need for pastors to self-insure in case they find themselves victims of sudden position loss. The advice, per Mikkelsen, was that every home should work toward at least three to six months of expenses put back in a financial security fund or savings account. Mikkelsen states, "When we first meet with a potential new client the first part of the process is to gather information in order to assess the whole financial picture of the client, which includes savings, debt, etc. From there we determine the client's goals and objectives." This is a process every pastor should undertake. In a sense the pastor is building their own severance, which is important considering the severance statistics revealed earlier in this chapter relating that most severances fell short of what was needed to bridge the gap between ministries. Mikkelsen suggested putting back as much as possible per month until the expense savings goal is reached and a severance savings account is built up. The pastor can even put this savings into an account that will generate some sort of interest but can be accessed in case of employment emergency. If the pastor does not find himself in need of this fund at any time in their ministry, then they will find themselves ahead in the retirement planning game. The pastor hopes to never have need of this fund until retirement but will be very grateful to have it when forced from a ministry. I cannot stress enough the fact that alleviating the economic impact to any degree after an event like this is paramount to the success of the healing process. The chances are that you will need this fund at some time in your ministry.

This leads to another point and issue: pastors must strive to be debt-free so that they can put a plan such as this in place. Many have used Crown Financial or Dave Ramsey to achieve debt-free status; however, pastors must be diligent to reach this milestone, which will greatly decrease the pain of job loss and the ability to achieve self-insuring status.

The next step is to have a plan in place and know what to do when job loss occurs. The two industry leaders in budgeting, debt management, and financial independence and security from a Christian perspective are Dave Ramsey and the Crown Financial Group. These two entities have many resources I have encouraged church members to use and even taught in a small group setting. However, one failure of my own and many pastors is failing to use these resources for themselves. These two entities have clear plans to follow in order to implement what they consider a crisis budget in the unfortunate case of any job loss, and in the case of Crown Financial, one can easily find fill-in-the-blank budget worksheets to guide the process.

When implementing a crisis budget, there are five steps that one must consider, according to Crown Financial. Those steps are: 1) determine what monthly income is available, 2) make written commitments to live off the new income and incur no new debt, 3) prioritize expenses; 4) delay nonessential expenses, and 5) analyze and adjust monthly subscriptions or recurring expenses.[43] This last step is where I have found much relief by negotiating rates of certain bills, cutting back or cutting off any memberships and subscriptions, and deferring bills for a short time. Crown Financial also stressed the importance of finding temporary work, something, due to reasons discussed earlier, that many pastors fail to do.

Dave Ramsey's group echoes the same plan yet words it a bit differently. Ramsey's five steps in "How to Budget After a Job Loss" are: 1) focus on the four walls, which are defined as food, utilities, shelter, and transportation; 2) pause extra debt payments; 3) cut out all unnecessary expenses; 4) make money while unemployed; 5) use emergency funds as a last resort and realize that this is temporary.[44] I would only add one caveat to the use of the emergency funds as a last resort. I would not wait to use the severance savings account spoken of earlier. This account is for the express purpose of bridging the gap when no severance is given and should be pulled from first. The emphasis here is to find resources that are readily available and have a plan. Unfortunately, many of the pastors interviewed, including myself, did not have a plan, and it caused the recovery to be delayed and more painful. There is a quote that is attributed to many authors, from Founding Father Benjamin Franklin to management writer Alan Lakein, that says, "if you fail to plan, you plan to fail." The need is for pastors to plan in case of emergency and follow the plan precisely. Many resources exist, such as the two mentioned above, that will help a pastor walk through this trying time with much more economic prowess.

Pastors tend to quickly fall into the belief that it would never happen to them even though many know of close friends who have traveled this path. The economic plan is one that no pastor wants to employ but must be in place. The phenomenon of unjustified termination or forced resignation is a path that is difficult to walk through under any circumstances but adding economic burden and uncertainty makes it feel like an impossible hill to climb.

"As a pastor, it is so difficult to share your burdens with church members for fear that the information shared can be used later against you. Church members have no idea what pastors have to deal with. I had nowhere to turn for emotional support."

—A Wounded Pastor

chapter eleven
A STRATEGY FOR HEALING— EMOTIONALLY

The emotional damage that can and does happen as a result of unjustified terminations and forced resignations can be long-lasting and have negative ramifications for the pastor's family, his spouse, and even for next ministry he undertakes, providing that the pastor even gets to that point. I remember, as if it were yesterday, the moment I discovered that a deacon and another church member had started a rumor about my marriage. I was angry, stunned, sad, and about a thousand other emotions at the same time. I remember telling my wife that I would never trust another deacon again. God has softened that hurt in me a bit with the new ministry position I am in and with a group of very godly and humble deacons, but the sting is still there. I remember thinking many different times during the course of the event and even today, why are these people doing this? They are the ones who claim to be a believer and should know better! A hurt like this takes years to overcome.

The pastors who were interviewed detailed a vast range of emotional damage and pain caused by the event, depending largely on the severity of the event itself. What kind of damage is this phenomenon causing? This has been alluded to in previous chapters, but the interviews provided some direct evidence. Two of the pastors who walked through especially difficult and egregious circumstances at the hands of the church or antagonist leading the charge said the emotional pain and fallout from it affected their marriages quite negatively. Many of the pastors expressed difficulty in trusting

LEVEL TWO — Emotional Recovery

Economic Recovery — **LEVEL ONE**

people and withdrew from certain individuals in their next assignment. There was much difficulty in coping with the feeling that the church, or at least the antagonist, seemed to get away without any consequences for their actions while the pastor suffered. Some of the pastors tended to carry a sense of failure with them for years after the event, undoubtedly affecting their future endeavors. This also causes those who experience the phenomenon to wrongly question the call to ministry or reject the call outright, finding it easier or more desirable to do anything other than pastor. One must note the additional dimension that pastors feel toward their family members and the collateral damage done to spouses and children and their inability to protect or shield them from the pain and loss. Pastors also can be the last ones to seek help through this journey, and although this is not an exhaustive list of the emotional toll these pastors walk through, it must be carefully navigated or they become wounded leaders who cause damage in the next assignment.

A pastor must develop a plan to deal with the emotional pain and hurt that is caused by those within the church and the months of feeling attacked and pressured, usually the case leading up to the event. This portion, much like the complete strategy, is also in its infancy. However, several factors related to healing have emerged in the research and from what has been learned through the interviews.

First, pastors must develop a structure or support system and friendships outside of the church. The stories and data both pointed to the idea that those who had mentors or support outside the church in which they served could be more successful in reentry to ministry. Pastors must take the time to develop this even though the tendency is to think of church first. All through scripture God placed the greatest leaders with others to take the journey with them—Paul had Barnabas, Moses had Aaron, Jesus sent the disciples out in pairs to the ministry field, and so on. The enemy wishes to isolate pastors so that they are more easily attacked and at the very least discouraged. Pastors must learn that they are not good leaders if they are unhealthy leaders and a system of checks and balances with trusted people outside the church is imperative. As my seminary pastoral care and counseling professor stated often, "Every pastor needs a good counselor."

Pastors must also give themselves the permission to have a hobby or interests outside of ministry that give themselves a chance to turn off the ministry brain for a while. Let me give a personal illustration that covers both friendships outside of ministry and the hobby issue. I have discovered the joy of cycling over the past two years and I cannot overstate the value it has added to my healing journey. I have even named my trusty Giant road bike "Cheaper Than Therapy." I have found that I can shut out the voices clamoring for attention and truly find some times of peace while out on the road. My wife will even notice when I am getting a bit stressed with the rigors of ministry and bring me my cycling helmet and tell me it is time for some cycling therapy. Cycling has even turned into ministry, being able to witness to those in the cycling community while on group rides. This demonstrates that even our hobbies turn into ministry, but it is different than the normal pressures of pastoring. I can set goals and easily see them met—which is hard to do sometimes in the ministry setting, ride with a group and have some fellowship, or even set out on a solo ride. It is hard to take a ministry call when on the bike and it forces time away. I have had to learn to make time to ride so that I am fully healthy and invested in the times of ministry and in the pulpit.

Pastors must find what interests them and not feel guilty when they spend some time pursuing those things. I know that pastors must balance their time and all the objections that are going through the mind about there being too much to accomplish and not pastor to go around at this time, but if a pastor is not healthy, it does not matter how much time they spend in ministry pursuits. They will not be giving their best.

Secondly, the pastor must clearly understand the Biblical principle of forgiveness and letting the antagonist go. In Ken Sande's work, *The Peacemaker: A Biblical Guide to Resolving Personal Conflict*, he states:

> "Through forgiveness God tears down the walls that our sins have built, and he opens the way for a renewed relationship with him. This is exactly what we can do when we forgive as the Lord forgives us: We release the person who has wronged us from the penalty of being separated from us. We do not hold wrongs against others, do not think about the wrongs, and do not punish others for them. By making and keeping these promises of biblical forgiveness, you can tear down the walls that stand between you and your offender. You promise not to dwell on or brood over the problem or to punish by holding the person at a distance. You clear the way for your relationship to develop unhindered by memories of past wrongs. This is exactly what God does for us, and it is what he calls us to do for others."[45]

The ability to walk through the principles of forgiveness is a foundational step of the healing process, and unless the pastor completes this step, he will be a wounded and less than effective minister for the gospel. The pastors who successfully reentered ministry experienced a moment when forgiveness took place, and they were able to hold no ill will against the church where they experienced the termination or resignation. This may be a momentary realization or a slower process of walking through forgiveness, but it must happen. The enemy wants bitterness and anger to take root in the wounded pastor's heart. The question is, how do you know this is happening? The answer is easy here. The most telling sign is the emotion that comes up in the pastor's heart when you hear that deacon's name mentioned, or even run into someone with a similar name. When the pastor can remember the person's name or event without the physical effects of the anger and other emotions welling up, then forgiveness has begun to take root instead of the anger and bitterness. Pastors must also practice what they preach when they look at verses such as Ephesians 4:31-32, which tell us, "Let all bitterness and wrath and anger and clamor and slander be put away from you, along with all malice. Be kind to one another, tenderhearted, forgiving one another, just as God in Christ also has forgiven you." (NASB) Pastor, the forgiveness that is extended to those that created the pain and hurt in ministry is not even contingent upon them. Pastors must forgive simply because Christ has forgiven us! This is, in fact, turning the antagonist fully over to Christ to handle and then keeping our hands off of the situation. The end result of this forgiveness is peace and no longer carrying a burden that even pastors are not designed to carry. I turn often to the four promises of forgiveness found in Ken Sande's work *The Peacemaker* to remind me how to practice biblical forgiveness. Those promises are: 1) I will not dwell on this incident, 2) I will not bring this incident up again and use it against you, 3) I will not talk to others about this incident, 4) I will not allow this to stand between us or hinder our personal relationship[46]. I know that in the case of termination or resignation, having a relationship with the church or members who caused the pain is not an option, nor should it be, but these promises guide my thinking that I will not give the perpetrators any time or energy and allow healing to truly begin.

The third area of strategy and the most profound piece to emerge, in my opinion, is developing an idea of treating the pastors with the same approach as anyone who has been exposed to a traumatic life experience. I introduced the term Post Traumatic Spiritual Stress Disorder—adding the term spiritual to point to the application within the church—in earlier chapters, and this direction of thought was reinforced through interviews and follow-up conversations with the subjects of the study. Experiencing unjustified termination or forced resignation from a church, a body where, Biblically, one should not find this happening, is a very traumatic experience to those who experience it. This portion of the strategy, as it currently stands, is only an introduction to this approach and how it may help heal the emotional wounds that pastors carry for many years past the event.

Post-traumatic stress disorder (PTSD) is most widely known through the experiences of soldiers who return from battle and find themselves having difficulty reintegrating into civilian life. The interviews of the pastors, as well as my own experience, have revealed that many who have experienced the phenomenon of unjustified termination and forced resignation describe the experience as coming out of a battle. The pastors experience some of the same symptoms described by sufferers of PTSD, yet as the goal is return to ministry, they face the prospect of entering the same battlefield that caused the pain and suffering. Pastors may not arrive at fully diagnosable PTSD as a mental health disorder. However, that does not diminish the fact that the phenomenon is traumatic, and the inability to deal with the trauma is a major factor in the number of pastors who never reenter vocational ministry. Let me be very careful to point out that none of the pastors interviewed have been formally diagnosed with PTSD, yet several have expressed feeling many of the same symptoms, such as fixating on flaws, dismissing the positive, assuming, catastrophizing, using all or none thinking, making feelings facts, overgeneralizing, abusive labeling, blaming, making unfavorable comparisons, and having regrets.[47] All these symptoms or coping mechanisms handicap the pastor in future endeavors and are experienced by pastors at different levels. A fear of reaching out to or a lack of availability of counseling for pastors to work through these symptoms also exists.

One example of this is in managing PTSD triggers. In their work, *Loving Someone with PTSD: A Biblical Guide to Understanding and Connecting with your Partner after Trauma*, the authors define managing triggers in the following way:

> "A trigger is a person, place, thing, or situation associated with the trauma that sets off a PTSD symptom. Therapy can show constructive ways of managing the symptoms and the hope is that by increasing the control of the symptoms one can reduce their frequency and intensity."[48]

The interviews revealed the pastors experienced many of the physical ramifications that can be linked to PTSD when facing certain situations, such as the search team process, deacons' meetings, business meetings, and other areas of ministry in which most of the previous attacks took place. This caused lack of sleep leading up to the event, physical sickness symptoms leading up to the event, a racing of thoughts, and overreacting to certain stimuli, with no evidence the current situation would produce the same results as past occurrences. I still struggle today with certain scenarios in ministry that cause these symptoms to take place. Something as simple as a text or phone call, or a meeting, or simply two people talking in the back of the worship center, can remind me of past events. The hurt and symptoms come rushing back, even though it's been a few years now since the last event took place. I am learning to manage the triggers and approach these common situations from a Biblical counseling perspective. This has proven, at least by anecdotal experience, to be paramount for a successful return to ministry.

The first place to start in the managing of triggers is to win the battle of the mind. I have lost track of how many times I have seen something that should be very innocent, such as a conversation between two deacons at the back of the church, and everything in my brain is trying to tell me, "here we go again." I have had to train my brain to think correctly about the situation instead of thinking that they are obviously talking about me or planning my demise. Pastors must train themselves to know the difference between thinking about things through the trauma brain and thinking about things as they truly are. The first step in winning the battle of the mind is to never battle alone. I have given a few select individuals in my life, one being my wife, the ability to tell me when I am thinking out of the wrong brain. I admit that sometimes their admonition is frustrating, but it at least shocks me out of the thinking pattern I am currently in and causes me to evaluate the merits of the event or thought properly. Most times I realize that I am not viewing the situation correctly. This slowing of the process allows me to make calculated decisions based on fact and not what I think is true based on past experiences.

The second step is to again go to God's Word and take the Philippians 4:8-9 test on every thought and situation you face that tries to tell you danger or attack is coming. Philippians 4:8-9 tell us, "Finally, brethren, whatever is true, whatever is honorable, whatever is right, whatever is pure, whatever is lovely, whatever is of good repute, if there is any excellence and if anything is worthy of praise dwell on these things. The things you have learned and received and seen in me, practice these things, and the God of peace will be with you." (NASB) I have even gone as far as taking a piece of paper and writing a synopsis of the situation I am now facing and then making a list according to each piece of the test. Write down what is actually true about the situation, not what is perceived to be true, even through the circumstances. By the time the list is complete, it becomes more difficult to listen to the lies of the enemy, and the pastor can begin to make right decisions as to how to respond instead of fight or flight.

Winning the battle of the mind is the first and most important step in the healing process when a pastor suffers from PTSSD. Pastors must also here practice what they preach and take every thought captive, dismissing the lies of the enemy, and allow the healing peace of Christ to intervene. This will allow the pastor to finally deal with the source of the problems and not just the symptoms.

Once the battle in the mind is on the winning side, the question that emerges next in the emotional component is whether a strategy exists to combat the trauma that has been experienced by the pastor. The strategy proposed is a three-phase strategy based on the work *Recovery from Psychological Trauma*, by Dr. Judith Herman from the Cambridge Hospital in Cambridge, Massachusetts, a leader in the study and treatment of victims of trauma. The recovery strategy can be quantified in three stages: 1) the establishment of safety and overcoming the trauma, 2) the telling of the story and grieving the loss, and 3) the rebuilding and restoration stage of life and ministry.

The first stage is establishing the safety of the individual who has experienced the trauma and at least beginning the stage of overcoming the acute pain of the trauma. At this juncture the pastor will have already addressed or begun to develop a plan to address the economic factors that should lead to an ability to address the emotional component. The pastor will also, most likely, remove himself and his family from the location or the immediate context of the trauma, making him ready to address the event from an emotional standpoint. According to Dr. Hermann, this involves developing a personal road map of recovery, developing realistic and attainable goals to achieve the road map with a realistic time frame, learning how to regulate emotions and behavioral symptoms, tapping into sources of strength, and developing coping mechanisms.[49]

The second stage is being able to tell the story and grieve the loss. This is the point at which a pastor must reach out and find other pastors or counselors who can assist in the process. I was able to find a licensed counselor on staff at a church who readily agreed to meet and process the issues and trauma of the terminations and resignations free of charge, and I am greatly indebted to this man of God. This journey allows the pastor to process the trauma in a safe environment and walk through the five stages of grief as they apply to experience. Dr. Herman relates that one knows that this stage is successful when, "the person reclaims their own history and feels renewed hope and energy for engagement with life."[50] In short, the trauma is actually placed in the past and the pastor feels safe to move forward emotionally, beginning to trust again, and able to see their way into ministry, which leads to the third stage.

The third stage in the emotional recovery plan is to rebuild and restore. This is the stage where the traumatic event no longer plays a defining role in the life of the pastor. The pastor begins to regain trust, move into successful ministry, and effect change in their experience, no longer viewing the church or its members through the trauma or emotional hurt. The PTSD no longer controls the pastor. Dr. Hermann states, "Recovering from trauma does not mean that you will be completely free of intrusive thoughts or feelings, rather you will reclaim your life, love, and your authentic self."[51] The healing in this stage can be compared to the stages that one goes through when dealing with grief. The pastor moves through each stage basically like the following:
1. Denial and refusing to acknowledge they are a victim of trauma, then to
2. Bargaining or trying to convince themselves that it was not that harmful or causing any problems in their ministry or relationships, then to
3. Anger when the pastor acknowledges that they are a victim of a traumatic experience but the only emotion is bitterness and animosity towards the perpetrators of the trauma, then to
4. Sadness, where the pastor realized the hurt but it turns to a depression and a feeling of loss, then finally to
5. Acceptance, where the pastor realizes that this something that is forever a part of their life but it no longer defines who they are and how they act.

The final stage is when the pastor realizes that they have healed and the trauma will no longer affect their future ministries. There is much written about these stages of grief and pastors even counsel their church members through these stages. Pastors must realize here as well that the truth that is good for their people must also take root in their own lives and practice. Pastors, allow yourself to grieve the situation and move forward in the healing process.

Conclusion

Travis Bradberry and Jean Graves, in their work *Emotional Intelligence 2.0,* state in the chapter concerning self-awareness:

"Your hard-wired emotional reactions to anything come before you even have a chance to respond. Since it isn't possible to leave your emotions out of the equation, managing yourself and your relationships means you first need to be aware of the full range of your feelings, both positive and negative."[52]

The pastor who is forced out of a ministry has had to deal with rejection and pain caused by those who should know better. This causes a rewiring of the emotions and brain and when a pastor finds themselves in situations that can be perceived as similar to that which caused the hurt and trauma, the brain sends the panic signals and the symptoms of PTSD go into full swing and before they know it, anxiety is high and function is diminished. In short, it shuts the pastor down and all they can see and feel are negative emotions, which cause you to wrongly act and react.

The emotional healing must include a rewiring of the brain and emotions to see the truth of a matter instead of a "here we go again" mentality. This cannot be done overnight and cannot be done alone. Bradberry and Graves go on to say, "Facing the truth about who you are can at times be unsettling. Getting in touch with your emotions and tendencies takes honesty and courage. Be patient and give yourself credit for even the smallest bits of forward momentum." The beauty for the believer, especially the minister, is that we do not take this journey of self-reflection and taking stock of our emotions alone. We participate with the Holy Spirit to weigh and measure our emotions, see things as God sees them and His word tells us they really are, and then begin to line up our emotions with the truth. We then begin to find peace and safety.

Once we begin to heal emotionally, we then can take an honest look at our relationship with the Lord and how this trauma has affected us spiritually. We turn to that now.

"I was very angry at God for everything that happened. I realized that He is sovereign and has a plan, but I still don't feel like I can see that plan. I have had many blunt times of prayer, but He has been faithful. I have felt His presence and comfort."
—A Wounded Pastor

"At first, I was angry and felt like the Lord had abandoned me or that I had lost my call to ministry. I even felt like maybe I had been disqualified from ministry. As time went on, I came to be at peace and to see how the Lord was using that situation to bring me to the place I am today."
—A Wounded Pastor

chapter twelve
A STRATEGY FOR HEALING— SPIRITUALLY

Augustine said of God, "Thou has made us for Yourself, and the heart of man is restless until it finds rest in You." So far in this journey the pastor has worked on economic stability and emotional healing from the trauma that having lost a ministry can cause. The next step in the healing process is to take a direct and honest look at your relationship with the Father. Do you find that, like the wounded pastor above, you are angry with God? Do you question where God has taken you and whether or not you missed something along the way? Spiritual healing is paramount to finding true healing and passion for ministry. Pastors that do not take this step seriously in their journey of healing will find themselves handicapped in the next ministry assignment.

The spiritual component revealed that the path the pastors took was very much like the experiences detailed in Chapter 6 of this work in the life of King David. Many of the pastors expressed feelings of anger at the Lord, spiritual abandonment, or even feelings of losing the call to ministry, and disqualification from ministry. Other pastors expressed a deeper understanding of the Lord's sovereignty, His unchangeable nature, and a deeper intimacy with the Lord. One pastor described the spiritual state as "at the time of the incident I believe that I truly leaned upon God for strength and courage. I had no one else to lean on or turn to for help. I felt as if I had to be the rock in our family pretending or acting as though it did not really affect me, but deep inside I was destroyed." At least two of the pas-

tors were so wounded emotionally and spiritually that they have not even attended a church, and they expressed their relationship with the Lord as not being in a very good place.

The phenomenon of unjustified termination and forced resignation creates what Dr. Chuck Lawless, dean and professor at Southeastern Seminary, calls defeated pastors, and he relates nine characteristics that the pastor must overcome. Those characteristics are 1) that pastors have lost their vision, 2) they are angry, 3) they have lost hope, 4) they live in retreat, 5) they cast blame, 6) they have lost community burden, 7) they have dropped their own spiritual disciplines, 8) they wonder about their call to ministry, and 9) they don't look forward to Sunday.[53]

The strategy that the pastor employs must seek to answer these characteristics and restore spiritual vitality and strength. This strategy for spiritual renewal is very connected to the emotional component of the four-phase plan and many of the same approaches mentioned above in the emotional category will also provide comfort and growth in the spiritual realm. This is what led me to loosely base a spiritual strategy on the three-phase recovery strategy by Dr. Hermann under the emotional healing component and the recovery from psychological trauma. The three-phase strategy, adapted to the spiritual healing, is the establishment of spiritual safety, reading the story, and rebuilding and restoration.

The first phase is to establish spiritual safety, which is vital for the pastor to move from spiritual crisis mode to spiritually renewed foundation. The last phase of the emotional recovery strategy led the pastor to begin to think more clearly and honestly about the crisis and the trauma that had been experienced and allowed the pastor to no longer be controlled by the trauma. The same can be said spiritually in that the pastor must begin to dwell on the truths of God's Word concerning the situation and not on intrusive thoughts. Remember that winning the battle of the mind begins with understanding God's truth. What does God's Word say about those in ministry? Paul relates in 2 Corinthians 4:1 concerning his ministry, which was also wrought with rejections and challenges, "Therefore, since we have this ministry, as we received mercy, we do not lose heart." (NASB) Pastor, your ministry was given to you by the Lord and you have been called according to His good purpose and pleasure. The one who has placed you and called you will not forsake you even in this journey. David wrote Psalm 126 when he was fleeing from Absalom, and he states in verses 4-5, "I was crying to the Lord with my voice and He answered me from His holy mountain. I lay down and slept; I awoke, for the Lord sustains me." (NASB) The tendency during this time is for wounded pastors to neglect their simple walk with the Lord and to fail to be honest with the Lord concerning our view of His relationship with us during this valley. David, as we discovered in the earlier chapter, was very blunt and honest with his feeling toward the Lord but was also humbled and sought the Lord's teaching and admonition. If the wounded pastor will take the time to work through a few starting steps, then the walk with the Lord will be strengthened and you will be able to see your way past the hurt and anger to the balcony of Leadership development.

The first step in this phase is to go back to the Philippians 4:8–9 test on every situation, which allows the pastor to think through every situation from a more Biblical worldview instead of reading everything through current circumstances. I want to encourage the pastor in this area of healing to take pen and paper and deliberately walk through this step. Write down each section of this passage at a time starting with what is true and then underneath write down what is actually true about the situation you find yourself. Be careful here that you do not write down what the circumstances feel to be true but what God says is true about this. When this list is written then the pastor prayerfully moves to what is honorable, then what is right, and so on until the test is complete. This causes a pause and a correction in thinking and allows the pastor to hear more clearly God's heart and God's truth about this journey. Seeing life through the lens of God's truth begins to heal the hurt and damage that has been caused. The Philippians 4:8 test has caused, more often than not in my own practice, times of worship in which I begin to realize once again who God is and how much He cares for me. I realize that He has not forsaken me in my life and ministry.

The second component of finding spiritual safety is to seek help outside of the situation rather than internalize and retreat. Many resources exist to help with this, but the pastor must take the initiative to find them and use them. I found several resources useful to pastors to find spiritual safety during this time. Websites like expastors.com, careforpastors.org, and pastoralcareinc.com provide articles and research specific to hurting pastors. Books such as *Catastrophic Crisis* by Echols and England, *Leading with a Limp* by D. Allender, and *Surviving Friendly Fire* by Dunn provide tools for spiritual healing. The pastor can take advantage of local retreat centers, such as Shepherds Care Ministry in my area, or licensed counselors who are on staff at a local church, as referred to previously. The pastor, although wounded, must take the initiative to seek out and find these sources to find spiritual safety. I personally found an associate pastor at a local church with a background in counseling that agreed to meet with me for several months to process both the emotional and spiritual component of the healing and found this to be a key piece of my healing process. Pastors must not wait for help to come to them but seek it out and make it a priority.

Another component of this strategy is that conventions and denominations must do a better job at making retreats and counseling affordable and available. I have found some good retreat and counseling resources offered by different groups, but they proved to be so cost prohibitive that many pastors, especially victims of this phenomenon, simply cannot take advantage.

The second phase of the strategy is simply just reading the story. The pastor must go to God's Word and seek out Biblical examples, much like the story of David, to begin to notice how these heroes of the faith navigated similar waters. I spoke of this a bit in the previous phase of this strategy, but more can be stated now. Pastors must realize that the men of the Bible that were used by God in magnificent ways were also humans who struggled with sin, self, and trials. Look to their stories to see how they continued through ministry no matter the cost or what was done to them. The pastor must also go to more modern-day heroes of the faith, such as Mueller and Spurgeon, to see how they navigated ministry waters. Spurgeon's battles with depression and difficulty are well documented, as well as the steps he took to battle those demons. Though culture may be different from their day to ours, the lessons and principles they applied in ministry can be used today by other wounded pastors.

The third phase of the strategy is the spiritual rebuilding and restoration phase, wherein the pastor must renew his own spiritual disciplines and spiritual strength. One way this was accomplished by several of the pastors that I interviewed was to find a healthy church to simply be a member of during the interim away from ministry. This provided for them much needed spiritual nourishment and growth. The pastors were able to sit under good Biblical teaching and be spiritually fed. This grew, for some, into opportunities to teach small groups, fill the pulpit, and to plug back into ministry work, providing small successes that boosted confidence and reestablished calling. This also kept the pastors in the network of teaching and refining of their skills that led to some comfort in the next ministry position.

The main way back to spiritual health is the simplest and one that many pastors teach to their congregations, but which they are the last to put into practice. Pastors must be diligent and dogmatic in incorporating the spiritual disciplines into their personal lives both before and after a trauma takes place—but especially after—to regain strong spiritual lives. The best resource known to this project director is Dr. Don Whitney's *Spiritual Disciplines for the Christian Life*. This book walks the reader through several of the main and most vital spiritual disciplines for the believer and offers guidance in putting these things into practice.

Conclusion

I have heard it said many times that doctors make the worst patients and I believe this thought carries over to the pastoral world. Pastors seem to be the worst when it comes to taking care of their own personal walk with the Lord. I am certain that this comes from the calling they have received to care for the flock and the practice of always putting the flock's needs ahead of their own. But this can be dangerous and detrimental not only to active ministry, but especially to the healing process. Jesus, on His earthly ministry, spent many times alone with the Father, even pushing away the demands of life and ministry for a moment. Jesus provides a model for pastors that we must take time alone with the Father, especially after a traumatic ministry experience. Rest in the Father's arms! Find healing and renewal spiritually! Then you will be able to learn some valuable lessons about ministry and leadership and be stronger than you have ever been.

"Good Shepherds must be patient, which I was not. Good Shepherds will not be looking for a way out, which I was at the time. Good Shepherds should not view their sheep as wolves, which I did constantly. Good Shepherds must preach faithfully and allow God to work, which goes back to being patient. Good Shepherds realize that it takes two to tango and they must be willing to acknowledge their own weaknesses and faults."

—*A Wounded Pastor*

chapter thirteen

BENEFITING FROM ADVERSITY
Becoming a Stronger Leader

The leadership development component has been set up by this project as the intended goal, or the landing spot, as one progresses through the strategy. Many pastors have yet to arrive at the balcony of leadership development and be allowed to enjoy the view, which the interviews revealed and several pastors freely admitted. Others expressed leadership development lessons learned that, when put under scrutiny, fit more with a survival or protection mentality, which would be defined as simply making sure this does not happen again in the next assignment or determining not to be hurt again. The responses in this category were "don't trust deacons ever again," "identify the Jezebel as soon as possible," and "be prepared for consequences every time you talk." These are reactions based on pain and seeking self-preservation instead of an honest look at one's leadership to see what can be changed. This is understandable to a certain degree and only adds weight to the necessity of the healing strategy so that one can truly participate in leadership development.

This is not to say that no leadership lessons were learned in the process. Many of the pastors were able to reflect back and

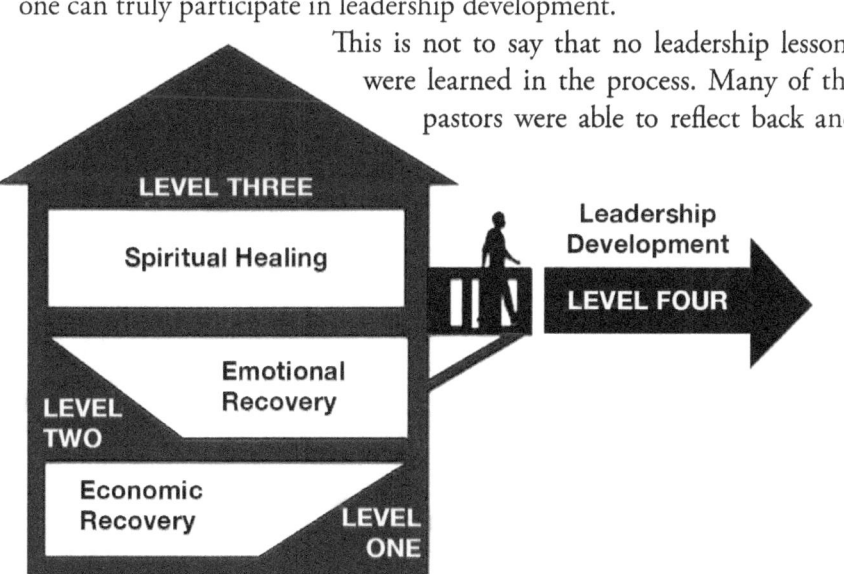

see that they may have pushed the vision too quickly, pursued education before seeking partnership with the church in the endeavor, lacked patience, or relied on unnecessary urgency while making changes. Several pastors expressed lessons learned in communication and having clear written expectations, starting with the search process and moving into actual ministry leadership. Another important aspect is the vital nature of outside mentors and godly friends. The interviews revealed that pastors who had a better support group tended to heal better and reenter ministry.

The goal for a leadership development strategy is captured well by what Echols and England say in *Catastrophic Crisis*:

> "The goal for leadership is not to be limited to the past. To use the vase illustration, God can take the broken pieces of a catastrophic crisis and, with some additional ingredients, recast it into something new. Although the new normal may elicit the memory of the old, it is something beyond the old."[54]

This quote captures the plight of the pastor and this phenomenon and what was found in the interviews. Many of the pastors remained chained to the past, unable to move forward. The crisis can be paralyzing, leaving pastors unable to complete the leadership learning process. One must incorporate the experience, along with good teaching and mentoring, to develop stronger leaders willing to face ministry again. Leadership development must be a recasting, honoring the old while creating the new leader.

A vast array of leadership information and authors exists to teach the pastor the necessary leadership lessons. Books like *Preventing Ministry Failure* by Wilson and Hoffman, *Failing Forward* by John Maxwell, and *Spiritual Leadership* by Blackaby are must reads for pastors who have experienced the phenomenon of being forced from ministry, not to mention the plethora of secular training on leadership. I have already written of the importance of mentorship and co-laborers in the emotional and spiritual component, which are no less important to leadership development; leaders need someone to journey with them in leadership. The pastor must take teaching or knowledge, plus their experiences, plus mentorship or coaching, to develop themselves into better leaders. Eric Geiger and Kevin Peck describe this as the "Development Convergence,"[55] in which the leader combines the experiences of the crisis with knowledge of leadership principles and godly mentoring or coaching so that essential leadership development can take place. Pastors must take the time to refocus, refine, and reevaluate their callings to ministry, as well as time to get to the point of developing a skill set that would weather the storm more successfully through the three components of experiences, knowledge or truth, and godly mentoring. When pastors journey through the economic, emotional, and spiritual strategies, they will begin to see what they went through in a different light, and with the help of coaching and great teaching, they will be better leaders for the ministry.

Conclusion

The biggest lesson personally learned through this process is how to pastor unafraid. I have personally walked through the complete process detailed in this project and was forced to walk the path with no road map. There was no guide to lead the way and warn of pitfalls to avoid. Even now ministry is not without challenges, and my philosophy of ministry is vastly different than that of the seminary student I was so many years ago. The pain and hurt is still there lurking in the shadows. The ability to trust and face certain ministry components is still difficult, but the healing has begun. God has used a part of the Body of Christ to heal some of the damage caused by those who claimed to be the Body of Christ and who have positioned themselves as leaders of the church. This student of God's Word and His church is beginning to learn how to pastor unafraid.

Chapter 1 stated that the prevailing question was whether enough information could be gleaned from the pastor's perspective to yield a complete view of the problem and whether a strategy could be developed from that view. The answer to this question is yes, but with a caveat. This problem has come into focus more clearly, yet more work needs to be done. This project has furthered the research to a substantial degree, and more is known of the landscape that pastors face. However, more needs to be done to build roads into this forest to bring the strategy to its fullest potential. I have already begun the work of expanding each level of the strategy to be able to put out companion pieces to further help wounded pastors. I desired, with this project, to reach into the phenomenon of unjustified termination and forced resignation and put a voice to the humanity it affects, while developing a structure upon which a strategy can be built. I believe that I have succeeded here; however, the work has only begun. This will continue to be a lifelong exploration for me, hoping that more pastors will find the same healing and return to ministry or at least no longer find themselves suffering from the wounds they carry. There are many challenges pastors face in the scope of ministry that are understood and even welcomed. This phenomenon is one that should not be found in the field of pastoral ministry and it has gone unexplored for far too long. May the journey continue, and may the solution be found. May we continue to heal and make sure that *nemo resideo*, no man be left behind.

Tell Your Story**

My fellow Wounded Pastor,

 I stated in the earlier chapters, that telling your story is an integral part of healing and taking the first step forward and I want to give you that opportunity. I pray that this will not only help you in your journey but also be able to be used in the future to build this body of research and help others that find themselves walking this path.
 Please go to the Wounded Pastor Blog at www.thewoundedpastor.wordpress.com and there you will find a tab labeled "Tell your Story". You will find a series of prompts to help you share your story as well as some direct questions to assist in the research portion of this project.
 Thank you for helping me further the research and for taking the first step in your journey of healing.
 I pray for you all,

Dr. Matthew Tanner

"At the time of the incident I believe that I truly leaned upon God for strength and courage. I had no one else to lean on or turn for help. I felt as though I had to be the rock in our family pretending or acting as though it didn't really affect me, but deep inside, I was destroyed."

—A Wounded Pastor

chapter fourteen

FOR COACHES AND MENTORS
Is Anyone Else Writing About This Phenomenon?

The process of writing this work has included unnumerable conversations with pastors and church leaders to which one question is asked in almost every conversation. What books are out there that can help a pastor in this journey? Why can I not find anything written about this subject to put in their hands to help? This book was written in order to provide an answer to that question, however, in my research I have come across a few resources that I would recommend to the wounded pastor or to the coach or mentor that is guiding them. This is a brief synopsis of what you will find in these resources.

There have been a small number of books written concerning the healing process that a pastor must go through, how to conduct the pastoral interview, how to navigate the pastoral search process, and even when to know it is time to voluntarily leave a current assignment. However, the scholarship available seems to touch very little on the phenomenon of being forced from a ministry position. My experience, which is backed up by a few industry leaders,[56] is that not many have tackled the subject of unjustified forced resignations and terminations to date. There have been some individual ministries, scattered throughout the Unites States, that are geared toward helping pastors who find themselves victims of this phenomenon and I continue to discover them often. The scope of these ministries is quite localized or simply priced to the point that many pastors who are dealing with the economic woes of unjustified termination or resignation cannot take advantage of their resources. The culmination of this chapter is a brief review of what could be found in this area of study. As I stated above, I have spoken to several who have attempted to help a wounded pastor and each of them have stated to me that it has been difficult to find resources to put in the hands of victims of unjustified termination and forced resignation, so I have included what I have found thus far. I will attempt to simply relate what these resources are about while allowing the reader, if they choose, to pursue these resources, make their own decision about their value to the subject at hand.

Review of Literature

Moving On – Moving Forward by Michael Anthony and Mick Boersma

The premise of this work is determining a goal for where one in professional ministry wants to be and then helping to lay out a plan on how to reach that goal. The author's intended audience is those in the ministry who have not yet left their current assignment but are desiring to leave for any number of reasons. In this work, the authors only mention briefly those who have been forced out of the office of pastor or those who have left the ministry altogether and have become, in their words, "casualties of a harsh and unforgiving world."[57] They, like many of the authors, are dealing with the outskirts of this subject and are choosing to deal only with the least difficult of circumstances.

Anthony and Boersma take the reader through a journey that may be likened to traveling abroad by plane and attempting to land the reader safely on the other side. The authors do give the reader three chapters that deal with the personal hurt and issues that leaving a ministry may cause; however, the bulk of the work details how to consider one's ministry calling and how to navigate the pastor search process. The only offering of help to those wounded by ministry or those in the transitional period is found in Chapter 10, which is little more than a list of helpful ministries with their websites and a retelling of another's work on this issue. The main idea of Chapter 10 of this work is simply to help the minister decide whether to "hang up the collar,"[58] which by their definitions is quitting ministry altogether.

Anthony and Boersma's work can be a useful resource for the Wounded Pastor. The minister who is wondering whether it is time to leave a current ministry for any reason or who is contemplating retirement may find resources here that are valuable to him. The pastor who has been unjustifiably forced to resign or terminated for unbiblical cause will not find as much to use, in my opinion.

Detour: Outliving Termination by Dr. Mike Hawkins

This work, by Dr. Hawkins, is a personal testimony of his experience in walking through the journey of an unjustified termination by a church. Hawkins admits in the preface that this work is not concerned with trying to determine why the event happened but is only concerned with the experiences after the termination. The stated purpose of this work is twofold: first, to "befriend those who have been hurt by termination," and second, to "demonstrate God's guidance in his life."[59] Hawkins does a very good job of meeting those expectations while detailing some of the highlights of the journey that was forced upon his ministry.

Hawkins first details the way the event happened, as well as the suddenness of its arrival in his journey. Chapter 1 catches the reader up to how the unjustified termination took place and is very similar to the stories previously explored by this author. Eighteen years of this pastor's ministry was ended with one vote. There was no explanation, no reasoning, just an abrupt and meaningless end. Hawkins confirms, in this journey that is his book, that the four main obstacles that were faced in his journey are the same categories that have been identified by this author as the emotional, economic, and spiritual components of the struggle and then being able to learn leadership lessons once the previous three components were addressed. Each of the subsequent chapters of this work detail Dr. Hawkins personal journey of finding answers concerning the economic hardship, wrestling with the emotional and spiritual toil such a journey leads a minister on, and finally learning some leadership lessons in the latter chapters that would prove both healing and necessary for future ministry success.

Hawkins' work follows the same path as my personal experiences and the experience of others, and it confirms the importance of the focus on economic recovery, emotional healing, spiritual healing, and leadership development. Hawkins' life experience, as written in this work, proved valuable as both confirmation of the direction of the book you are currently reading and as a rubric as to the development of the interview process, and as a useful interview in its own right. This is also one of the only works of its kind that I have found and it is vastly under-distributed.

Surviving Friendly Fire: How to Respond When You are Hurt by Someone You Trust by Ronald Dunn

Ronald Dunn is one of the few authors who have at least attempted to deal with the issue of those who have been hurt by those within the church who should have been trustworthy. Dunn uses the term "friendly fire" to refer to those within the church being wounded by others in the church who should have been on the same side. Although dealing with any relationship in the church in which this phenomenon has been experienced, this work is not specific to the pastor/church relationship that is the scope of the current project. However, Dunn at least begins the conversation related to this problem.

Dunn, in the prologue of the book, rightfully explains that the scope of the problem is most likely worse than what is reported to institutional and denominational agencies. Dunn speaks of the scope of the problem as being like that of the military and the cases of "friendly fire" being around two percent in combat. Within the church it has been found to be admittedly around five to seven percent, yet Dunn rightfully states that if the true numbers were known, they would be likely to be much greater than this.

Dunn has separated the work into three parts, first defining and developing what "friendly fire" is, secondly detailing how the reader is to survive being a victim of "friendly fire," and lastly offering a treatise on forgiveness, which is detailed as the way to return "friendly fire."

Dunn attempts to define a cause for this phenomenon in the church as a death and failure of integrity within the membership of the church, the subject to which Chapter 1 is entirely devoted. I believe that it is a correct assumption and definition but only one piece of a convoluted puzzle. "Friendly fire," according to Dunn, is a failure of relational integrity and a loss of community and a triumph of those who engage in unity-threatening behavior. Dunn is correct in stating that a loss of integrity breeds a loss of duty, honor, and loyalty, which then fractures community.[60] The churches have become individualized in focus and are no longer Biblical in many of their practices and relationships. Decisions are constantly made about what is right for the individual and not what is right for the body or what is Biblical. Integrity is one facet of the many reasons that are cause for "friendly fire," and the interviews thus far have supported the premise that there are many other reasons and issues at play. It is difficult to narrow it down to just a lack of integrity and community or rampant individualism.

In Chapter 2, Dunn details the "view from the pit," which is described as the current church culture, when he states, "When a pastor finds himself in trouble, whether it is his doing or not, he often discovers that many he thought were friends were not. His family is ostracized by the very people they once socialized with."[61] This is the very experience I have been through with unjustified terminations/resignations. Once difficulties ensue in the church, it seems as if the pastor is the most expendable and little is cared for his well-being or that of his family. Dunn ends the chapter with a few illustrations from those who have survived this phenomenon in the church. These stories are exactly like the ones found thus far in this project, which proves the existence of the problem in churches today.

Dunn spends Chapter 3 detailing for the reader the effect trauma has on the victim of "friendly fire" and briefly discusses how to make sure that past hurts do not needlessly shape future endeavors. The truth remains that the abused must not become the abuser and that our future must be met once healing takes place. However, one is almost always affected in some way by the circumstances in the past, and rather than simply moving on, a strategy must be implemented that makes one stronger even with the trauma of the past.

Chapter 4 attempts to describe and identify the "spear throwers," who are defined by Dunn as those who are the ones firing the shots in the "friendly fire" scenario. The background causes, such as jealousy, insecurity, mistrusted motives, personal ambition and others listed by Dunn, are quite accurate; however, the list of motives for these kinds of attacks is as numerous as the sins man can invent. Dunn aptly describes the actions of the antagonists in this chapter. Where Dunn makes a mistake is when he indicates in this chapter that "God will deliver you from 'friendly fire' if you react righteously in the situation."[62] This, in my opinion, is simply not true all the time. This is a dangerous absolute to put forth by stating that, so long as the victim of "friendly fire" is acting godly enough, then he will be rescued from the situation. The many cases recorded in Scripture, the interviews I've conducted thus far with other pastors, and my own personal experience indicate that no matter how godly the actions on the victims' part, they are required to walk through the difficulty and are not rescued from it. The rescue that was prayed for and longed for simply did not arrive. Part of God's plan was for them to walk through the difficulty, not for them to be rescued from it.

Chapters 5–7 introduce the reader to the steps to take when one becomes a victim of "friendly fire." Dunn asserts that since churches are imperfect places filled with imperfect people, being mistreated is simply going to happen and not much is suggested as to whether or even how this phenomenon can be avoided. There is no view on how to keep "friendly fire" from happening in the church or even a suggestion that this is possible, but the reader is left only with the encouragement just to act like Christ when it does happen.

Chapter 8, called "Unmasking Idols," does get into and does a very good job of detailing the important step of making sure that, as a victim of "friendly fire," one does not make the situation worse by adding their own sin to the mix. Getting the log out of one's own eye is a step that must be taken to ensure that one does not bring any fire or unnecessary attention to a ministry that welcomes "friendly fire." In a sense, the minister must do all he can not to create a situation where it makes it easy to be fired upon. Dunn goes too far when he equates anxiety with an idol being present in a person's life and when he indicates that the only way to alleviate anxiety is to rid oneself of the idols.[63] Anxiety cannot be defined so simply, and its causes are multifaceted. One can remove all idols of the heart and still suffer from anxiety, especially when one's livelihood is removed by the "friendly fire." Business meetings and other church meetings can become hotbeds of anxiety as the minister is constantly watching for where the fire is going to come from next. Sometimes anxiety builds simply because someone is a victim of the sins of others and has nothing to do with that person harboring an idol in their heart.

Dunn then moves to teaching the reader the important truth of being able to see the hand of God working even through "friendly fire" and the difficulties of ministry and church life. Dunn is correct here in that the healing process must include being able to see God work in the little things and building upon those things as God brings complete healing. The statement is made correctly that it is hard to see the providence of God through tears and grief.[64] I could not agree more with this statement, and this statement is the very reason this book was written. When the person can deal with the economic issues to stabilize the situation and then deal with emotional and spiritual healing, one can begin to see God's hand at work, which leads to a stronger future. This is the scope of the strategy being developed by this project.

Part three of this work outlines the teaching and truth of forgiveness. Dunn defines for the reader exactly what forgiveness is and how the reader who has been a victim of "friendly fire" can gain freedom through forgiveness. The author does well enough with the issue of forgiveness; however, it is simply one step of many that the reader must take to regain full health after a "friendly fire" incident. Issues such as regaining trust, learning leadership lessons, and protecting oneself from future incidents are not examined in this work.

Conclusion

I anticipated that this section would be lacking in available resources, yet this is a topic that is discussed in the seminary classroom, the coffee shop, and in many different conversations between pastors. There is almost a sarcastic joking that is interjected into the conversation that hopes to help the pastor who has entered into the club of those who have arrived as a pastor and (in a sense) earned their proverbial stripes by becoming a victim of unjustified forced termination and resignation. However prominent this subject is in the conversations of pastors of local churches, the scholarly world has been notably silent. As stated above, there are some who have hinted at the subject, but up to this point, none have attempted to make at least a beginning in the development of a strategy to help these pastors begin to heal. The fact that more needs to be done has been made painfully clear by the lack of literature to include in this very review.

appendix a
WRITTEN INTERVIEW GUIDE

Name
Thank you for taking the time to give me your story. I pray that the information gathered here will prove vital to those who may have to walk the path of unjustified termination or forced resignation in the future.

Please fill out the steps of this guide and sign the confidentiality agreement and return as soon as possible.

The purpose of this interview is for you, the Pastor/Ministry Leader, to share your story of unjustified forced termination/resignation: This is defined as:

> This process, affecting many pastors and church leaders, is defined in at least two ways. It is first defined as, "the process by which a congregation, a personnel committee, or individual leader within a church terminates or forces a minister from a position of ministry."[65] Secondly, it is defined from the pastor's perspective as getting to the point that the pastor abdicates his post, "due to the constant negativity found in personal attacks and criticism from a small faction within the congregation from whom the minister feels psychologically pressured to step down from his service of ministry."[66]

Please feel free to share as much or as little of your story as you deem pertinent to allow this project director to begin to develop a strategy that will help future pastors and ministry leaders to successfully reenter ministry in a stronger and much more healthy manner.

The names of the church, individuals involved, as well as your own information will be held in the strictest confidence and will in no way be made public.

I have included bullet points to guide you in this story telling process to ensure that all areas are covered. Please consider these are you write your story.

Simply tell what happened
Tell your story of unjustified resignation or termination which may include but is not limited to, the call to the specific ministry, what led up to the problem, what was the catalyst that caused the end of the ministry, etc..

Please use the following bullet points to guide the story telling. You may add any details that you may feel are relevant to the story.

- Tell your story of unjustified forced termination or resignation.
- What did you do to survive financially? (economic component of strategy)
- What actions did you take on your journey to cope with the event and/or heal emotionally?
- How did this event affect or change your relationship with God?
- Have you been able to identify leadership lessons that were learned during this process?
- Are you currently still in ministry? IF not, what vocation are you in?
- Is your current ministry similar to the ministry in which the event took place?
- If you are currently in another ministry, detail the path that you took back into ministry.

Quantitative Data questions
(event is defined as the moment when the unjustified or forced termination/ resignation took place)

Level of Education when event took place?
(ranging from no formal education through earned Doctoral degree)

Years of Ministry experience when event took place?

Denominational affiliations of church where event took place?

What ministry position did you hold?

What was the approximate size of the congregation where event took place?

Did you spend any amount of time away from ministry after the event and if so how much?

What was your age when event took place?

Did you get a severance package after the event and if so how much in terms of months or weeks salary?

Did you have a mentor or another pastor that guided you through the process of the event as if so was this person inside the church or outside the church where event occurred?

appendix b
QUANTITATIVE DATA

	Level of Education	Years of Ministry Experience
P1	Bachelors (MDiv in progress)	15
P2	DMin	39
P3	MDiv	15
P4	MDiv	17
P5	DMin	13
P6	DMin	15
P7	MDiv	30
P8	MDiv (DMin in progress)	30
P9	MDiv	11
P10	Bachelors	12
P11	Bachelors (MDiv in progress)	17
P12	MDiv	30
P13	Bachelors	15
P14	DMin, ThD (2 Doctorate)	28
P15	MDiv	1
P16	MDiv	3
P17	MDiv (PhD in progress)	4
P18	Master of Arts Pastoral Studies	1
P19	Master of Arts (2nd Masters in progress)	12
P20	MDiv (PhD in progress)	8
P21	MDiv	5
P22	Bachelors (MDiv in progress)	9
P23	Bachelors	4
P24	Bachelors (MDiv in progress)	5
P25	MDiv	6
P26	MDiv	34
P27	MDiv	4
P28	MDiv	11
P29	MDiv (DMin in progress)	14

	Denominational Affiliation	**Ministry Position**
P1	Southern Baptist	Assoc. Pastor
P2	Southern Baptist	Lead Pastor
P3	Southern Baptist	Lead Pastor
P4	Southern Baptist	Lead Pastor
P5	Southern Baptist	Lead Pastor
P6	Southern Baptist	Student Pastor
P7	Southern Baptist	Lead Pastor
P8	Southern Baptist	Lead Pastor
P9	Southern Baptist	Youth and Family Pastor
P10	Southern Baptist	Lead Pastor
P11	Southern Baptist	Youth and Worship Pastor
P12	Southern Baptist	Lead Pastor
P13	Southern Baptist	Lead Pastor
P14	Southern Baptist	Lead Pastor
P15	Southern Baptist	A/V Technicion, pastoral intern
P16	American Baptist	Assoc. Pastor
P17	Southern Baptist	Assoc. Pastor
P18	General Baptist	Lead Pastor
P19	General Baptist	Lead Pastor
P20	Southern Baptist	Lead Pastor
P21	Southern Baptist	Lead Pastor
P22	Southern Baptist	Assoc. Pastor
P23	Southern Baptist	Lead Pastor
P24	Southern Baptist	Assoc. Pastor
P25	Southern Baptist	Lead Pastor
P26	Southern Baptist	Lead Pastor
P27	Southern Baptist	Lead Pastor
P28	Southern Baptist	Assoc. Missionary
P29	Southern Baptist	Lead Pastor

	Approx. Size of Congregation	**Time away from Ministry**
P1	150	few months
P2	125	5 months
P3	120	3 years
P4	400-500	6 weeks
P5	250	none
P6	300	4 months (still out of ministry)
P7	120	18 months
P8	30	none
P9	250	13 months
P10	170	4 years (still out of ministry)
P11	275	none
P12	120	18 months
P13	100	2 years
P14	60	no longer in ministry
P15	600	none
P16	225	none
P17	200	none
P18	90	15 months
P19	85	3 months
P20	120	6 months
P21	100	10 years
P22	300	5 months
P23	60	6 months
P24	50	none
P25	150	few months
P26	100	4 months
P27	120	6 months
P28	n/a	none
P29	70	1 year

	Age (when event took place)	Severence
P1	36	none
P2	64	9 months
P3	44	6 months
P4	61	6 months
P5	41	none
P6	32	2 months
P7	60	9 months
P8	62	none
P9	33	3 months
P10	46	none
P11	38	3 months
P12	60	9 months
P13	40	3 months
P14	55	2 weeks
P15	28	1 month
P16	30	1 month
P17	31	none
P18	32	none
P19	40	2 weeks
P20	40	3 months
P21	30	unknown
P22	47	4 weeks
P23	26	none
P24	23	none
P25	28	6 weeks
P26	56	6 months
P27	31	6 months
P28	37	none
P29	41	6 months

	Mentor (inside or outside of church)
P1	pastor: outside
P2	pastor: outside
P3	mentor, pastor: outside
P4	none
P5	none
P6	mentor: inside
P7	pastor: outside
P8	none
P9	mentor: outside
P10	none
P11	children's pastor, elders: inside
P12	friend, pastor: outside
P13	none
P14	none
P15	youth pastor: inside
P16	none
P17	friend: outside
P18	none
P19	pastor: outside
P20	pastor, friend: outside
P21	none
P22	none
P23	friends: inside
P24	none
P25	none
P26	none
P27	mentor, pastor: outside
P28	mentor, pastor: outside
P29	mentor, pastor: outside

appendix c
FURTHER RESEARCH AND DATA

"What is the phenomenological study method and how does it serve the issue of unjustified forced terminations and resignations?" Let us seek to answer this question now.

A Brief History of Phenomenology

The phenomenological method of research as it is known today is a fairly new method of research, which has its beginnings as far back as the early 1900s. Although early researchers of human thought and behavior (Christoph Friedrich Oetinger, Immanuel Kant, and Johann Gottlieb Fichte) mentioned some forms of phenomenology in their writings, the discipline of phenomenology did not appear in mainstream study until the early 1900s. Edmund Husserl, in his work *Logical Investigations*, launched phenomenology as a method of research in the field of psychology in his attempt to find logical progression in the field of understanding human thinking. In this work Husserl attempted to develop and define phenomenology as:

> "... the scientific study of the essential structures of consciousness. By describing those structures, Husserl promises us, we can find certainty, which philosophy has always sought. To do that, Husserl describes a method—or rather, a series of continuously revised methods—for taking up a peculiarly phenomenological standpoint, 'bracketing out' everything that is not essential, thereby understanding the basic rules or constitutive processes through which consciousness does its work of knowing the world."[67]

Husserl would spend his life's work and study refining the art and practice of phenomenology. Many considered Husserl to be the father of this study method and maintained "... that it was primarily meant to study how individuals describe and experience matters through their senses."

However, phenomenology did not appear as a popular method of research until around 1994, when Dr. Clark Moustakas authored the work *Phenomenological Research Methods*. Moustakas held the viewpoint that research should focus on the "wholeness of experience and a search for the essence of experiences," and he viewed experience and behavior as "an integrated and inseparable relationship of a phenomenon within the person experiencing the phenomenon."[68] Since Moustakas's groundbreaking work on phenomenology as a research method, several schools of phenomenology have arisen and its practice has become more accepted in the world of scientific research.

Phenomenological Study Method in the Field of Unjustified Forced Terminations /Resignations

The next question that must be asked is whether this method of research has been employed in the area of unjustified forced terminations and resignations before. The answer to that is, yes, but only in a very limited fashion.

In 2017 Dallas and Sheila Speight published a piece entitled, "Exploring the Lived Experience of Forced Termination Among Southern Baptist Clergy Couples: A Retrospective Study."[69] The work that was completed by the Drs. Speight proved, for me, a foundational piece for the current study being undertaken and the only such study of its kind. I remember running through the house with excitement telling everyone how excited I was to find this article. The piece sets the stage for the phenomenological study in the current field of pastoral termination and resignation, as well as reiterates some ideas and definitions already put forth in the current project.

Drs. Dallas and Sheila Speight interviewed a total of ten couples to gain direct input as to their experience of forced termination. The couples relayed their story of forced termination and what was learned from those stories filled the basis of the article written, which is in practice slightly different than the method of phenomenological study. The bulk of the article then details their findings from this very small sample size, which in fact support the findings already stated in this project.

The article begins with defining the issue of forced termination and brings out the valid point that there used to be a day when clergy were respected and valued in the community yet are now faced with increasing pressure and challenges not previously seen. The definition of forced termination used in this article is "the result of a process of involuntary removal of paid and non-paid clergy persons that results from a period of traumatic and demeaning psychological and emotional abuse."[70] The question that must be raised and has been alluded to in this project is what does this abuse cause in the lives of those that fall victim to it? Speight notes that those who have experienced involuntary or forced termination as a result of "mobbing" causes the pastors to experience "increased relationship problems, reduced well-being, suicidal behavior, and in the most extreme cases, Post Traumatic Stress Disorder."[71] I have experienced personally many of these symptoms and believe this experience is one reason a strategy for healing must exist.

Even though there has been some research on the fact that the problem exists and is proving dangerous to the ministers that face it, the authors clearly state in the first page of the piece that little has been done on this issue to help the victims of this kind of abuse:

> "… to date, researchers have focused on topics such as high-risk congregations, church conflicts, causes of forced termination, stress and burnout, well-being outcomes of clergy, and forced termination, yet **missing is a study into the retrospective experiences of clergy and spouses related to forced termination**. The long-term influence of forced termination on the clergy and spouse has not been determined. Though the existing literature revealed painful experiences of clergy related to forced termination, **missing is an awareness of how such experiences change or influence clergy and their spouses and least three or more years following the incident.**"[72] (emphasis mine)

The Drs. Speight also state that "Forced Termination among clergy is a prevalent and life changing experience yet has received little scholarly attention."[73]

In the section on consequences of forced terminations, the Speights emphasize that, because of the autonomy of the churches, these pastors face financial strain, coupled with poor prospects for finding resources to help. Only 35.2%[74] of those who have experienced forced termination receive a severance package, and pastors are not eligible for unemployment benefits, which means that 75%[75] would not survive financially four months after termination. Other consequences of this phenomenon are the questioning of the pastor's call to ministry with the previously stated finding that many of the pastors who are forced to resign or are terminated in this way never go back into ministry. These pastors, after termination or resignation face increased relational problems and issues with trust, depression, intense anxiety, and guilt, indicating that 71% of clergy and their families had difficulty trusting anyone following a forced termination.[76]

I have found this to be painfully true, which leads to the reason the subject has been undertaken. As the Drs. Speight state, "what might alter such events from occurring in the future is yet to be determined. However, faith groups have an opportunity to study this matter further and develop a strategy to address it from several aspects including education, intervention, and support."[77]

Extra Charts

Question Three: What was the denominational affiliation of the church where the event took place?

The third chart, Denominational Affiliation (Figure 3), yielded no real surprises. The great majority came from Southern Baptists, understandable considering the nature of the project, the methodology by which the interviews were procured, and the fact that I am a Southern Baptist

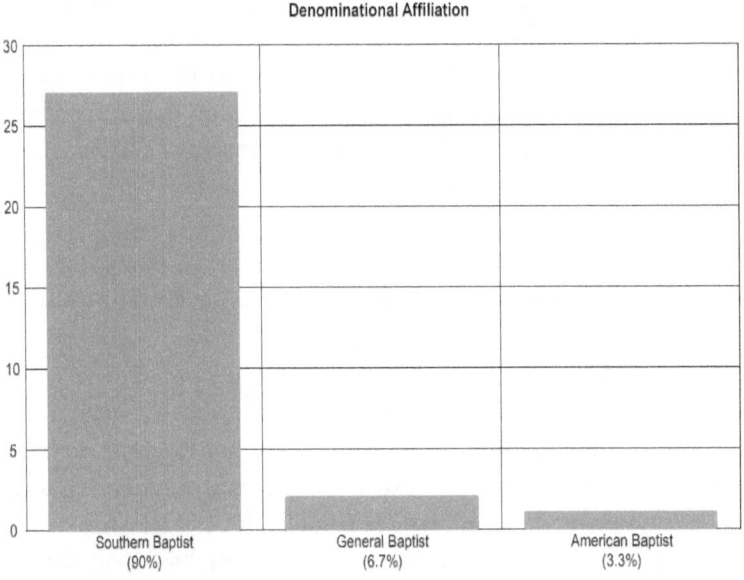

Figure 3

pastor. Several appeals were made to other denominations and those outside of my personal and denominational networks that yielded no results or interviews. Perhaps more could have been done in this area, but the nature and sensitivity of the phenomenon and information dictated that the existence of at least a passing relationship, through myself personally or through a mutual connection, had to be established in order for the information to be given. Simply put, cold contacts yielded no results.

Question Four: What ministry position did you hold?

The fourth chart, Ministry Position (Figure 4), also yielded little information to be analyzed. Most interviews were from the lead pastoral position; however, care was taken to make certain some results were outside of this singular position to demonstrate that this phenomenon does take place in all areas of ministry position, though perhaps for different reasons. In the case of the associate positions, this director found that instead of misplaced leadership within the church, the antagonistic leader often

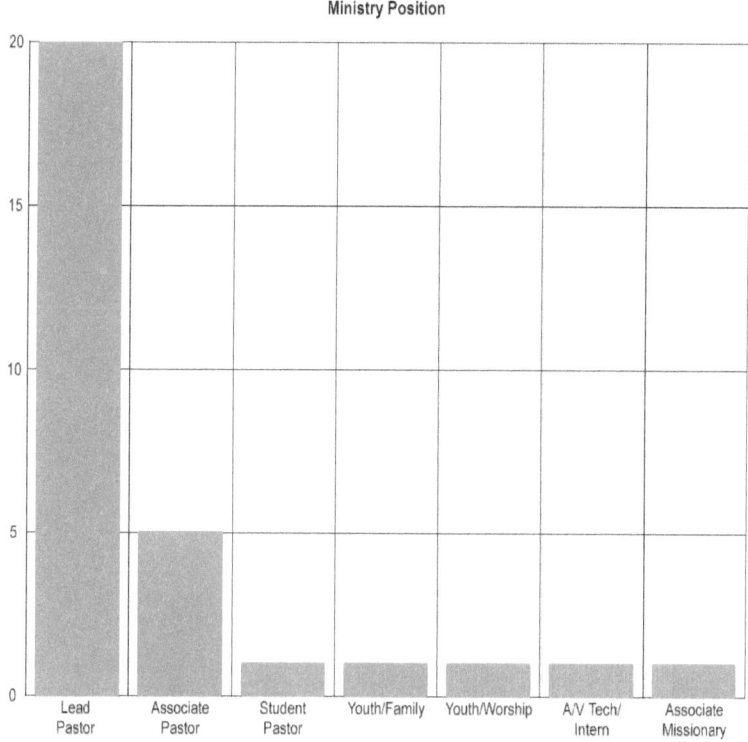

Figure 4

was a lead pastor engaging in toxic leadership. In some cases, manipulative or paranoid leaders caused the phenomenon to take place. This is not unlike the antagonistic deacon who usurps leadership authority over the pastor, as some of the same heart issues are in play- they only hold different offices. One interesting fact is that even lead pastors can develop the same bad leadership issues discovered in the church leaders who position themselves in wrong leadership roles, which should cause any researcher not to place all of the fault for the phenomenon in one area alone.

Question Seven: What was your age when the event took place?

The next category, the age of the pastor when the event took place (Figure 8), did not reveal much more information than has already been dealt with in the length of ministry experience category. This category, to be correctly understood, must be reviewed in conjunction with the length of ministry to better understand the ramifications and just where this information would lead. The reality is that this phenomenon is not a young man's issue or due to a lack of experience but both a ministry and life experience issue. This can happen at any time and at any age in a pastoral career. Some in the older category who experienced the event found it harder to deal with some of the issues, mainly economic, due to the fact that many churches resist calling a pastor so close to "retirement"

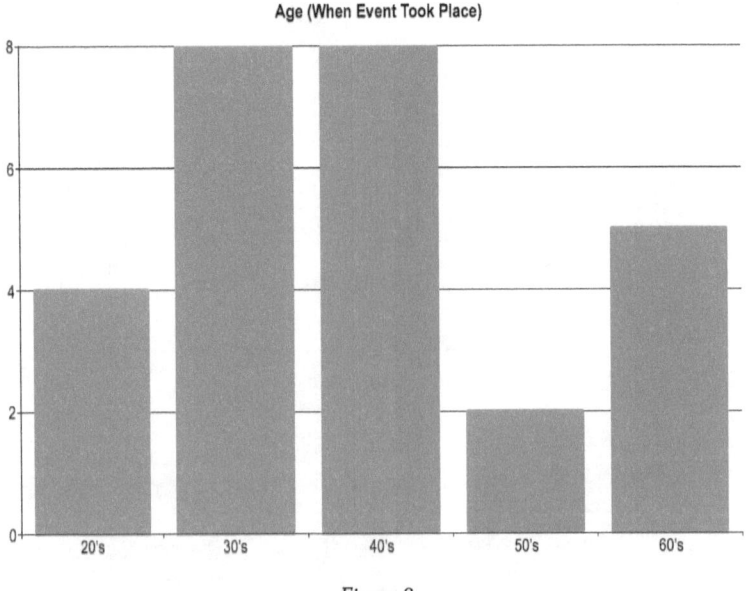

Figure 8

age, which undoubtedly factored into whether they made it successfully back into ministry vocationally.

Final Thoughts

What I learned from my research?

At the beginning of my project, my theory was that it would be possible, through the interviewing of pastors, to develop a strategy to assist pastors in the healing process and successful reentry of ministry. The results of the project itself lead to a determination of partial success and a determination of more that needs to be done. The data clearly shows that this phenomenon is an intrinsic problem within the church that must be navigated better by the pastors themselves. The four stages of the proposed strategy have been shown to be the correct stages of the healing process and in the correct order; however, this strategy is still at its beginning stages. Perhaps more interviews or more research into the lives and experiences of the pastors will lend credence to the information obtained thus far and further develop a more complete strategy in the future.

Prospects for Future Study

The prospects for future study have been mentioned in the different areas of the strategy analysis but will be listed in a more direct formal manner at this point in the project. There is a definite need to gather more interviews to develop the strategy in a complete manner.

I was successful in tripling the number of those interviews from victims of the phenomenon; however, this is still a little-studied problem that needs to be addressed.[78]

Another topic for further study is to take a look at the phenomenon from the church's perspective, something intentionally left out of this project, to see what, if anything, can be learned from the church's point of view as to the cause or solution to this problem. This will be a very difficult undertaking due to the autonomy of the local church and the intrinsic difficulty in finding the information, but it could yield interesting results. The idea of treating this phenomenon in pastors in the same manner as those treated with diagnosed PTSD would assist the strategy in ways that could not be counted. I believe this to be a vital part of the healing strategy that should be quantified and studied further.

The final aspect of strategy is to take a second or third journey into the whole phenomenon. I hope that pastors who read this book will be willing to share their story so that the healing strategy can develop more completely and a network of wounded but healing pastors can grow. The more that can be learned about this strategy and the more that this phenomenon can be given attention, the closer pastors will be to having a strategy to assist in healing and reentry into ministry. Churches need healthy pastors who will stay the course and the bleeding must be stopped and this problem fixed.

The following areas of future study were identified and hope to be studied in the future to a greater degree:

- Study and identify certain parameters of severance pay and develop a guide that would assist churches and pastors in determining appropriate severance pay, especially in the event of unjustified termination and forced resignation.
- Develop a guide, possibly as a companion to the strategy developed in this study, to guide mentors in counseling those who have been through the phenomenon of unjustified termination and forced resignation.
- Study the churches where pastors have been unjustifiably terminated or forced to resign in order to have a better understanding of the phenomenon, to see what may be contributing to the phenomenon, and to develop a strategy for churches to use in healing and moving forward.
- Study and develop a strategy for a pastor who has been called to the church as pastor who has recently been through the phenomenon in order not to repeat the event again.
- Study the reason why there were no cases or victims of the event who went back into ministry during the six to twelve month range, whether or not the ones who were out of ministry past the one year mark were more successful in reentry to the pastor position and more successful at the new location, and what may have allowed some to go back into ministry more quickly than six months and whether those cases were successful over time.
- Develop a study of each of the individual common characteristics and identifiers of the phenomenon as they happen in the church and what strategy can be built to combat the issue.

BIBLIOGRAPHY

Books

Allender, Dan B. *Leading with a Limp: Take Full Advantage of Your Most Powerful Weakness.* Colorado Springs, CO.: WaterBrook, 2008.

Anthony, Michael J., and Mick Boersma. *Moving On—Moving Forward: A Guide for Pastors in Transition.* Grand Rapids, MI: Zondervan, 2007.

Bragan, Janis, and Wesley D. Balda. *Handbook for Battered Leaders.* Downers Grove, IL: IVP Books, 2013.

Barfoot, D. Scott, Bruce E. Winston, and Charles Wickman. "Forced Pastoral Exits: An Exploratory Study" (2005): 19.

Battenhouse, Roy W. (Roy Wesley). "The Tragedy of Absalom: A Literary Analysis (2 Samuel 13–18)." *Christianity and Literature* 31, no. 3 (1982): 53–57.

Blackaby, Henry T., and Richard Blackaby. *Spiritual Leadership: Moving People on to God's Agenda, Revised and Expanded.* Revised edition. Nashville, TN: B&H Books, 2011.

Briggs, J R. "Transforming Failure: How God Used a Painful Season of Ministry to Change My Life." *Leadership* 35, no. 2 (2014): 21–24.

Briggs, J.R. *Fail: Finding Hope and Grace in the Midst of Ministry Failure.* Downers Grove, IL: InterVarsity Press, 2014.

Burns, Bob, Donald Guthrie, and Tasha Chapman. *Resilient Ministry: What Pastors Told Us About Surviving and Thriving.* Downers Grove, IL: IVP Books, 2013. Accessed October 11, 2018.

Cionca, John R. *Before You Move: A Guide to Making Transitions in Ministry.* Grand Rapids, MI: Kregel Academic & Professional, 2004.

Cleaveland, Adam Walker. "Pastoral Transitions in the Age of Social Media." *Congregations* 40, no. 3–4 (2013): 29–32.

Crow, Greg. "Region, Role, and Size as Risk Factors in Clergy Attrition" (March 26, 2010).

Dunn, Ronald. *Surviving Friendly Fire How to Respond When You're Hurt By Someone You Trust.* Nashville, TN: Thomas Nelson, 2001.

Echols, Steve F., Allen England, and David S. Dockery. *Catastrophic Crisis*. B&H Academic, 2011.

Elkington, Robert. "Adversity in Pastoral Leadership: Are Pastors Leaving the Ministry in Record Numbers, and If So, Why?" *Verbum et Ecclesia* 34, no. 1 (February 28, 2013). Accessed January 16, 2019. http://verbumetecclesia.org.za/index.php/VE/article/view/821.

Fearon, H. Dana, and Gordon S. Mikoski. *Straining at the Oars: Case Studies in Pastoral Leadership*. Grand Rapids: Eerdmans, 2013. Accessed October 16, 2018.

Frisbie, David. *Managing Stress in Ministry*. Kansas City, MO: Nazarene Publishing House, 2014. Accessed October 16, 2018.

Gallagher, T. "Fired! Do Church Employees Get Unemployment Benefits?" *National Catholic Reporter: The Independent News Source*, 2009.

Geiger, Eric, and Kevin Peck. *Designed to Lead: The Church and Leadership Development*. Nashville, TN: B&H Books, 2016.

Goodwin, E, "Forced Terminations and Ethics," *The Servant*, Publication of Ministering to Minsters Foundation Inc., 2.

Hall, Heidi. "HARD JOB, HIGH CALLLING: Reports of Clergy Attrition Are Often Exaggerated, but Pastors Still Face Daunting Challenges." *Leadership* 37, no. 1 (2016): 44–48.

Hawkins, Mike. *Detour: Outliving Termination*. Lee's Summit, MO: Father's Press, LLC, 2009.

Hicks, Donald Quentin, "A Study of the Conflicts within Churches that Lead to the Termination of Pastors within the Southern Baptist Convention, Accompanied by a Proposal of Preventive and Interventional Solutions" (2010). *Doctoral Dissertations and Projects*. 408

HERMAN, J.L. (1998), Recovery from psychological trauma. *Psychiatry and Clinical Neurosciences*, 52: S98-S103. doi:10.1046/j.1440-1819.1998.0520s5S145.x

Herman, Judith. *Trauma and Recovery: The Aftermath of Violence—from Domestic Abuse to Political Terror*. New York: Basic Books, 1997.

Husserl, Edmund. "Phenomenology—Edmund Husserl." Accessed October 14, 2019. https://science.jrank.org/pages/10639/Phenomenology-Edmund-Husserl.html.

Jansen, Julie. *I Don't Know What I Want, But I Know It's Not This: A Step-by-Step Guide to Finding Gratifying Work, Fully Revised and Updated*. Revised, Updated edition. New York: Penguin Books, 2016.

Lane, Richard J. "David's Escape from Absalom." *Journal of Interdisciplinary Studies* 27, no. 1–2 (2015): 139–154.

Lore, Nicholas. *The Pathfinder: How to Choose or Change Your Career for a Lifetime of Satisfaction and Success.* Touchstone Books, n.d. Accessed October 16, 2018.

Larue, J.C, "Forced Exits: A Too Common Ministry Hazard," *Christianity Today International*, 42.

Mathewson, Steven D. (Steven Dale), Carey Casey, and Dee Duke. "Faces of Change: Three Stories of Pastors Who Grew through Transition." *Leadership* 18, no. 1 (1997): 57–60.

Matsakis, Aphrodite. *Loving Someone with PTSD: A Practical Guide to Understanding and Connecting with Your Partner After Trauma.* The New Harbinger Loving Someone Series. Oakland: New Harbinger Publications, 2014.

Maxwell, John C. *Failing Forward: Turning Mistakes Into Stepping Stones for Success.* Reprint edition. Princeton, NJ: Thomas Nelson Publishers, 2007.

McCarter. "II Samuel," *Anchor Bible*. Vol. 9. Garden City, NY: Doubleday, 1984.

McKenzie, Steven L. *King David: A Biography*. Gale Virtual Reference Library. New York: Oxford University Press, 2000. Accessed May 1, 2019.

Moeller, Bob. "Grating Expectations." *CT Pastors*. Accessed October 16, 2018. https://www.christianitytoday.com/pastors/1996/winter/6l1031.html.

Oates, Wayne E., and Wayne E. Oates. *Grief, Transition, and Loss: A Pastor's Practical Guide.* Creative pastoral care and counseling series. Minneapolis: Fortress Press, 1997.

Oswald, Roy. *Running Through the Thistles: Terminating a Ministerial Relationship with a Parish.* Lanham, MD: Rowman and Littlefield, 1978.

Powell, Thomas. "Forced Terminations Among Clergy: Causes and Recovery," Liberty University, 2008.

Roach, David, "Pastoral Termination Common but Often Avoidable, Experts Say." *Baptist Press*. Accessed February 21, 2019. http://www.bpnews.net/43286/pastoral-termination-common-but-oftern-avoidable-experts-say.

Roehlkepartain, Eugene C. "Ministry Focus: Pastors in Transition." *The Christian Ministry* 18, no. 1 (January 1987): 7–18.

Rowell, Jeran. "Ministerial Attrition: When Clergy Calls It Quits the Relationship of Superintendents and Pastors." 20. ANSR Conference, 2010.

Ruff, Michael. "Post-Traumatic Stress Disorder: A Biblical Counseling Perspective." The Master's College, 2015.

Sande, Ken. *The Peacemaker*, 3rd edition. Baker Books, 2004.

Shelley, Marshall, and Jim Berkley. "THE PASTOR PARACHUTE." *CT Pastors*. Accessed October 16, 2018. https://www.christianitytoday.com/pastors/1990/summer/90l3016.html.

Simon, Marilyn K, and Jim Goes. "Phenomenological Research" (n.d.): 5.

Simpson, Timothy F. "Not 'Who Is On The Lord's Side?,' But 'Whose Side Is The Lord On?': Contesting Claims And Divine Inscrutability In 2 Sam 16:5–14" (n.d.): 186.

Smith, David Woodruff. "Phenomenology." In *The Stanford Encyclopedia of Philosophy*, edited by Edward N. Zalta. Summer 2018. Metaphysics Research Lab, Stanford University, 2018. Accessed January 22, 2019. https://plato.stanford.edu/archives/sum2018/entries/phenomenology/.

Speight, Dallas E., and Sheila W. Speight. "Exploring the Lived Experience of Forced Termination Among Southern Baptist Clergy Couples: A Retrospective Study." *Journal of Psychology & Christianity* 36, no. 2 (Summer 2017): 149–160.

Spencer, J Louis, Bruce E Winston, and Mihai C Bocarnea. "Predicting the Level of Pastors' Risk of Termination/Exit from the Church." *Pastoral Psychology* 61, no. 1 (February 2012): 85–98.

Spencer, J., Bruce Winston, and Mihai Bocarnea. "Predicting the Level of Pastors' Risk of Termination/Exit from the Church." *Pastoral Psychology* 61, no. 1 (February 2012): 85–98.

Stewart, Kristin. *Journal for the Liberal Arts and Sciences 13(3) 112 Keeping Your Pastor: An Emerging Challenge*, 2009.

Tanner, M, J.N Wherry, and A.M Zvonkovic. "Clergy Who Experience Trauma as a Result of Forced Termination." *Journal of Religion and Health* 52 (2013): 1281–1295.

Toler, Stan. *Stan Toler's Practical Guide for Ministry Transition: How to Navigate Pastoral Change Personally and Professionally*. Indianapolis, IN: Beacon Hill Press, 2010.

Tripp, Paul David. *Dangerous Calling: Confronting the Unique Challenges of Pastoral Ministry*. 1st edition. Wheaton, IL: Crossway, 2012.

Turner, Chris, "Control Issues Head List for Pastoral Terminations." *SBC Life*. Accessed February 21, 2019. http://www.sbclife.net/article/2137/control-issues-head-list-for-pastoral-terminations.

Vander Hart, Mark D. "Being Christlike in Conflict: Perspectives from the Old Testament." *Mid-America Journal of Theology* 27 (2016): 111–121.

Vensel, S.R. "Mobbing, Burnout, and Religious Coping Styles among Protestant Clergy: A Structural Equation Model and Its Implications for Counselors." Dissertation, Florida Atlantic University, 2012.

Walls, Thomas R. "Pastors in Transition: Why Clergy Leave Local Church Ministry." *Missiology* 34, no. 3 (July 2006): 421–422.

Weitzman, Steven. "David's Lament and the Poetics of Grief in 2 Samuel." *The Jewish Quarterly Review* 85, no. 3/4 (1995): 341–360.

Whitney, Donald S., and J. I. Packer. *Spiritual Disciplines for the Christian Life*. Enlarged-Revised edition. Colorado Springs: NavPress, 2014.

Wiggins, Alexandra R. "Lost in Transition." *Nurse Leader* 14 (June 1, 2016): 219–221.

Willis, C. "Terminations of Pastors, Staff Leveling off, Survey Results Show." *Baptist Press*, 2001.

Wilson, Michael Todd, and Brad Hoffmann. *Preventing Ministry Failure: A Shepherd Care Guide for Pastors, Ministers and Other Caregivers*. Downers Grove, IL: IVP Books, 2007.

Wind, James P. "Pastors' Untold Stories: A Silence That Begs to Be Broken." *Congregations* 31, no. 4 (2005): 5–5.

Wolfelt, Allen. *Healing After Job Loss: 100 Practical Ideas*. Fort Collins, CO.; Lancaster: Companion Press, 2010.

Electronic Sources

"I & II Samuel: A Commentary." Accessed June 4, 2019. http://eds.b.ebscohost.com.libproxy.mbts.edu/eds/ebookviewer/ebook/bmxlYmtfXzg0OTMxMV9fQU41?sid=ef6c23cb-6446-4db3-aeab-96c7a1013c96@sessionmgr102&vid=26&format=EB&rid=130.

"Are You a Defeated Pastor? Here Are 9 Characteristics." 2016. *ExPastors* (blog). December 14, 2016. http://www.expastors.com/are-you-a-defeated-pastor-here-are-9-characteristics/.

"Ask Chuck: Implementing a Crisis Budget." 2020. *Crown* (blog). April 10, 2020. https://ww.crown.org/blog/ask-chuck-implementing-a-crisis-budget/.

"DIOTREPHES The 1st Century Tyrant—3 John 9–12" Milton Dunavant Accessed June 11, 2019. http://churchgrowth.cc/Diotrephes.htm.

"How to Budget After a Job Loss." n.d. Daveramsey.Com. Accessed June 8, 2020. https://www.daveramsey.com/blog/budgeting-after-job-loss.

"Insider's Guide to Finding a Job." *Overdrive*. Accessed October 16, 2018. https://www.overdrive.com/media/75744/insiders-guide-to-finding-a-job.

"Ministerial Transition." *Faith and Mission* 10, no. 2 (1993): 3–61.

"Pastor In Transition 50 Ppl." *US Official News*, 2014.

"Statistics on Pastors." Dr. Richard J. Krejcir, http://www.intothyword.org/apps/articles/?articleid=36562.

The Stanford Encyclopedia of Philosophy, edited by Edward N. Zalta, Summer 2018. Metaphysics Research Lab, Stanford University, https://plato.stanford.edu/archives/sum2018/entries/phenomenology/.

"The Strange World of SBC 'Small' Churches." *SBC Voices*, William Thornton, Last modified March 7, 2017. Accessed May 18, 2020. https://sbcvoices.com/the-strange-world-of-sbc-small-churches/.

"What Is the Nature of Pastoral Authority? — Perspectives from a Methodist, a Presbyterian, and a Baptist." *9Marks*. Benjamin Merkle, Accessed July 15, 2019. https://www.9marks.org/article/what-is-the-nature-of-pastoral-authority-perspectives-from-a-methodist-a-presbyterian-and-a-baptist/.

"These 7 Practical Tips Will Keep Pastors Encouraged and Healthy in Ministry." 2018. *ExPastors* (blog). April 2, 2018. http://www.expastors.com/7-ways-pastors-can-stay-encouraged-and-healthy-in-ministry/.

ENDNOTES

[1] The previous known number of cases studied was 8–10 in Drs. Speights' work highlighted previously in this chapter. This initial work proved vital in the construction of the interview process as well as the whole of the project. The goal of this project was to further the research in a significant manner.

[2] J.C LaRue, "Forced Exits: A Too-Common Ministry Hazard," *Christianity Today International*, 42.

[3] E. Goodwin, "Forced Terminations and Ethics," *The Servant*, Publication of Ministering to Ministers Foundation Inc., 2.

[4] I have no intention of taking away from the ministries that have worked diligently to take care of the many wounded pastors that have come from the world of ministry. Groups such as Johnny Hunt's Care for Pastors (www.careforpastors.org), and many like them have done a wonderful work. The problem still exists on a grand scale. and my remarks above are an attempt to simply show the gravity of the problem and the need for a larger scale strategy and solution.

[5] I am speaking in terms of the broader Evangelical church because studies and statistics, which will be dealt with at a later point in the dissertation, show that this is not only a Southern Baptist issue. My personal experience with this phenomenon is strictly Southern Baptist, but in the project phase, it is the hoped to gain interviews and insight from all circles of the Evangelical Church.

[6] Chris Turner, "Control Issues Head List for Pastoral Terminations," *SBC Life*, http://www.sbclife.net/article/2137/control-issues-head-list-for-pastoral-terminations.

[7] David Roach, "Pastoral Termination Common but Often Avoidable, Experts Say," *Baptist Press*, http://www.bpnews.net/43286/pastoral-termination-common-but-oftern-avoidable-experts-say.

[8] These reasons mentioned just now are either personal examples or were relayed to me by brothers in ministry.

[9] Turner, "Control Issues Head List for Pastoral Terminations."
[10] The project phase of this work will be a phenomenological study and will be explained in more detail in Chapter 4. For now, the phenomenological study is the study of structures of consciousness as experienced from the first-person point-of-view. The central structure of an experience is its intentionality, its being directed toward something, as it is an experience of or about some object. David Woodruff Smith, "Phenomenology," *The Stanford Encyclopedia of Philosophy*, edited by Edward N. Zalta, Metaphysics Research Lab, Stanford University, Summer 2018, https://plato.stanford.edu/archives/sum2018/entries/phenomenology/.
[11] Thomas Powell, "Forced Terminations Among Clergy: Causes and Recovery," dissertation, Liberty University, 2008.
[12] "Reasons for Attritions Among Pastors, A Quantitative Report, Pastor Protection Research Study," Lifeway Research, http://lifewayresearch.com/wp-content/uploads/2015/08/Reasons-for-Attrition-Among-Pastors-Quantitative-Report-Final1.pdf.
[13] I have examined both the 2015 and the 2008 report from Lifeway Research and have found that the results are similar.
[14] Michael Todd Wilson and Brad Hoffman, *Preventing Ministry Failure* (Downers Grove, IL: Intervarsity Press, 2007), 31.
[15] Robert Elkington, "Adversity in Pastoral Leadership: Are Pastors Leaving the Ministry in Record Numbers, and if so, Why?" *Verbum Et Ecclesia*, 34, www.dx.doi.org/10.4102/ve.v34i1.821.
[16] *How Many Quit? Estimating the Clergy Attrition Rate*, Into Action, www.into-action.net/research/many-quit-estimating-clergy-attrition-rate/ accessed Nov 20, 2018.
[17] Scott Barfoot, Bruce Winston, and Charles Wickman, "Forced Pastoral Exits: An Exploratory Study," The School of Leadership, Regent University.
[18] J. Louis Spenser, Bruce Winston, and Mihai Bocarnea, "Predicting the Level of Pastor's Risk of Termination/Exit from the Church," *Pastoral Psychology* 61 (2012): 85–98.
[19] Robert Elkington, "Adversity in pastoral leadership," 34.
[20] "The Strange World of SBC 'Small' Churches," *SBC Voices*, March 7, 2017, https://sbcvoices.com/the-strange-world-of-sbc-small-churches/.
[21] These assumptions were largely based upon my own experience and the data concerning the scope of the problem detailed in Chapter

1 of this project. The rate of the phenomenon taking place in Evangelical denominations being approximately 3–7%, based on other research.

[22] "What Is the Nature of Pastoral Authority?—Perspectives from a Methodist, a Presbyterian, and a Baptist" n.d., https://www.9marks.org/article/what-is-the-nature-of-pastoral-authority-perspectives-from-a-methodist-a-presbyterian-and-a-baptist/.

[23] The prophecy is made as a response to Hannah's desperation in 1 Samuel 1:17–18. The response is found in 1 Samuel 1:19–20 when Samuel's birth is announced.

[24] Definition derived from Brown, Driver, Briggs Hebrew lexicon, Francis Brown, C Briggs, S.R. Driver, Hendrickson Publishers, Peabody MA., 1996

[25] Steven L. McKenzie, *King David: A Biography*, Gale Virtual Reference Library (New York: Oxford University Press, 2000), 154–175.

[26] P. Kyle McCarter, "II Samuel," *Anchor Bible*, vol. 9 (Garden City, NY: Doubleday, 1984), 344.

[27] Mark D. Vander Hart, "Being Christlike in Conflict: Perspectives from the Old Testament," *Mid America Journal of Theology* (2016), 117.

[28] All statements concerning David's emotional cries are taken from Psalms 3,5,43,145 (NASB).

[29] McKenzie, *King David: A Biography*, 170.

[30] Antagonist in the Church: How to Identify and Deal with Destructive Conflict, Augsburg Publishing House (Minneapolis MN, 1988) Pg. 25.

[31] "DIOTREPHES The 1st Century Tyrant—3 John 9–12 by Milton Dunavant," n.d., accessed June 11, 2019, http://churchgrowth.cc/Diotrephes.htm.

[32] Speight and Speight, "Exploring the Lived Experience of Forced Termination, 149–60.

[33] Vensel, "Mobbing, Burnout, and Religious Coping Styles among Protestant Clergy, 2012.

[34] Per email correspondence with Dr. Rich Houseal, Research Services, Nazarene Global Ministry Center, Lenexa, KS, March 27, 2019.

[35] Per phone call and subsequent follow up email with Dr. Franklin Dumond, director of congregational services for the General Baptist Convention, Poplar Bluff, MO, November 6, 2019.

[36] Per phone call and email with Scot McConnel, Lifeway Research Department, April 1, 2019.
[37] Per phone call and email with Sharon Casada, demographic specialist for the General Council of the Assemblies of God, October 30, 2019.
[38] "Reasons for Attrition Among Pastors," 10–12.
[39] Roach, "Pastoral Termination Common."
[40] Turner, "Control Issues Head List for Pastoral Terminations."
[41] Dallas E. Speight and Sheila W. Speight, "Exploring the Lived Experience of Forced Termination Among Southern Baptist Clergy Couples: A Retrospective Study," *Journal of Psychology & Christianity* Vol. 36, no. 2 (2017): 149–60.
[42] The information and plan was derived from a phone call and follow-up email with Robert Mikkelsen, certified financial advisor with the Cardinal Investment Group, Conway, AR.
[43] "Ask Chuck: Implementing a Crisis Budget," *Crown* (blog), April 10, 2020, https://www.crown.org/blog/ask-chuck-implementing-a-crisis-budget/.
[44] "How to Budget After a Job Loss," Daveramsey.Com, accessed June 8, 2020, https://www.daveramsey.com/blog/budgeting-after-job-loss.
[45] Ken Sande, *The Peacemaker*, 3rd ed., Baker Books, Grand Rapids, Mi, 1997 156–157.
[46] "Biblical Forgiveness Enables You to Forgive as God Forgave You" accessed March 16, 2021 https://rw360.org/biblical-forgiveness/
[47] Schiraldi, *The Post-Traumatic Stress Disorder Sourcebook*, McGraw Hill Companies, New York, NY, 2000, pg.162.
[48] Aphrodite Matsakis, *Loving Someone with PTSD: A Practical Guide to Understanding and Connecting with Your Partner After Trauma*, The New Harbinger Loving Someone Series (Oakland: New Harbinger Publications, 2014), 123–124.
[49] Judith L. Herman, "Recovery from Psychological Trauma," *Psychiatry and Clinical Neurosciences* (September 1, 1998), https://onlinelibrary.wiley.com/doi/abs/10.1046/j.1440-1819.1998.0520s5S145.x.
[50] Herman, "Recovery from Psychological Trauma," 9.
[51] Herman, "Recovery from Psychological Trauma," 9.
[52] Travis Bradberry and Jean Graves, *Emotional Intelligence 2.0*, (Talent Smart Inc., 2009) San Diego Ca. Pg. 61-62
[53] "Are You a Defeated Pastor? Here Are 9 Characteristics," *ExPastors* (blog), December 14, 2016, http://www.expastors.com/are-you-a-defeated-pastor-here-are-9-characteristics/.

54 Steve F. Echols, Allen England, and David S. Dockery, *Catastrophic Crisis* (B&H Academic, 2011), Nashville Tn. Pg. 164.

55 Eric Geiger and Kevin Peck, *Designed to Lead: The Church and Leadership Development* (Nashville, Tennessee: B&H Books, 2016).

56 The industry leaders alluded to include the chairperson of Lifeway Research and a leader in a seminary connected with the Nazarene denomination of churches, who have both stated that statistics and information concerning the scope of the project simply do not exist.

57 Mark Anthony and Mick Boersma, *Moving on--- Moving Forward* (Grand Rapids: Zondervan Publishers, Inc.) 2007, 11.

58 Anthony and Boersma, *Moving on--- Moving Forward*, 137.

59 Mike Hawkins, *Detour: Outliving Termination* (Lee's Summit, MO: Father's Press, LLC, 2009), Preface.

60 Ronald Dunn, *Surviving Friendly Fire How to Respond When You're Hurt by Someone You Trust* (Nashville, TN: Thomas Nelson, 2001), 7.

61 Dunn, *Surviving Friendly Fire*, 14–15.

62 Dunn, *Surviving Friendly Fire*, 46.

63 Dunn, *Surviving Friendly Fire*, 78.

64 Dunn, *Surviving Friendly Fire*, 92.

65 LaRue, "Forced Exits," 42.

66 Goodwin, "Forced Terminations and Ethics,", 2.

67 "Phenomenology—Edmund Husserl," n.d., accessed October 14, 2019. https://science.jrank.org/pages/10639/Phenomenology-Edmund-Husserl.html.

68 Marilyn K. Simon and Jim Goes, "Phenomenological Research," n.d., 5.

69 Speight and Speight, "Exploring the Lived Experience of Forced Termination," 149–160

70 M. Tanner, J. Wherry, and A. Zvonkovic, "Clergy Who Experience Trauma as a Result of Forced Termination," *Journal of Religion and Health* 52, 1281–1295.

71 S. R. Vensel, "Mobbing, Burnout, and Religious Coping Styles among Protestant Clergy: A Structural Equation Model and Its Implications for Counselors," dissertation, Florida Atlantic University, 2012.

72 Speight and Speight, "Exploring the Lived Experience of Forced Termination," 149–160.

73 Speight and Speight, "Exploring the Lived Experience of Forced Termination," 149–160.

[74] C. Willis, "Terminations of Pastors, Staff Leveling off, Survey Results Show," *Baptist Press*, 2001.

[75] T. Gallagher, "Fired! Do Church Employees Get Unemployment Benefits?" *National Catholic Reporter: The Independent News Source*, n.d.

[76] Barfoot, Winston, and Wickman, "Forced Pastoral Exits," 19.

[77] Speight and Speight, "Exploring the Lived Experience of Forced Termination," 149–160.

[78] The previous known number of cases studied was 8–10 in Drs. Speights' work highlighted previously in this chapter. This initial work proved vital in the construction of the interview process as well as the whole of the project. The goal of this project was to further the research in a significant manner.

ABOUT THE AUTHOR

Dr. Matthew Tanner was born in Belleville, Illinois to Dr. Steve and Mary Tanner in March 1977. Matthew and his identical twin brother, Joshua, were given a ten percent chance of surviving through the night. Trusting in the sovereign plan of God, their parents dedicated Matthew and Joshua's lives to the Lord, and both have lived healthy lives in service to the Lord.

Dr. Tanner grew up in both central and north Arkansas before graduating high school and moving to attend College of the Ozarks. It was there he completed a degree in Administration of Justice and Psychology. While attending College of the Ozarks, Dr. Tanner met his wife, Heather, and they have been married since 2002. The Tanners are proud of their three daughters: Sarah, Shelby, and Samantha.

After undergraduate school, Dr. Tanner attended Midwestern Baptist Theological Seminary and earned a Master of Divinity degree in 2006, a Master of Theology, and a Doctor of Ministry in December 2020.

Dr. Tanner has served as pastor for several churches in the state of Missouri, interim pastor for a church in South Dakota, and Director of Missions in his own ministry. He currently is, at the publication of this book, lead pastor of Northside Baptist Church in Bernie, Missouri.

Dr. Matthew Tanner

SCRIPTURAL REFERENCES

A
Acts 13:22 ESV 71
Acts 14:21-22 NASB 12
Acts 20:28 61

C
2 Corinthians 4:1 NASB 120

E
Eph. 4:11 61
Ephesians 4:31-32 NASB 112

J
3 John 1:9 81
3 John 1:9 NASB 80
3 John 1:10 81, 82
3 John 11 82

M
Matthew 18 31

P
Philippians 4:8-9 NASB 114, 121
Psalm 3:1-3 NASB 68
Psalm 3:1 NASB 74
Psalm 5:9 NASB 74
Psalm 42:6 NASB 74
Psalm 43:2 NASB 74
Psalm 51 75
Psalm 126: 4-5 NASB 120
Psalm 145 75

R
Romans 3 82

S
1 Samuel 1 62
1 Samuel 2:12 63
1 Samuel 2:22 63
1 Samuel 2:29 63
1 Samuel 2:33-34 NASB 66
1 Samuel 3:19 NASB 66
1 Samuel 8 64
1 Samuel 9:2 64
1 Samuel 14:24 65
1 Samuel 14:33 70
1 Samuel 15 65, 71
1 Samuel 61
2 Samuel 61
2 Samuel 4:4-5 72
2 Samuel 13 69
2 Samuel 13:19 NASB 69
2 Samuel 15:4-5 71
2 Samuel 15:7 71
2 Samuel 15:12 71
2 Samuel 15:30 73
2 Samuel 16:5-8 74
2 Samuel 16-17 72
2 Samuel 17 73
2 Samuel 17:1-4 74
2 Samuel 18 NASB 73

INDEX

A

Allender, D. 121
antagonist(s) 45, 62, 79, 80, 81, 82, 86, 110, 111, 112
Antagonists in the Church: How to Identify and Deal with Destructive Conflict 79
Anthony, Michael 132

B

Baptist Press 17
Blackaby, Henry T. 126
Blackaby, Richard 126
Boersma, Mick 132
Bradberry, Travis 117

C

Casada, Sharon 89
Catastrophic Crisis 121, 126
control issues 17, 20, 90, 91

D

Detour: Outliving Termination 132
Dumond, Dr. Franklin 89
Dunavant, Milton 81
Dunn, Ronald 121, 133, 134, 136

E

Echols, Steve 121, 126
economic issues/recovery 28, 93, 94, 98, 103, 133
Elkington, Robert 39
emotional healing/recovery 28, 93, 94, 98, 103, 109, 116, 117, 133

Emotional Intelligence 2.0 117
England, Allen 121, 126
Exploring the Lived Experience of Forced Termination Among Southern Baptist Clergy Couples: A Retrospective Study 150

F

Failing Forward 126
forced resignation 15, 17, 25, 37, 54, 76, 79, 82, 85, 91, 100, 101, 120
forgiveness 111, 112, 136
Franklin, Benjamin 107

G

Geiger, Eric 126
Graves, Jean 117

H

Haugk, Dr. Kenneth 79
Hawkins, Dr. Mike 132, 133
healing process 32, 40, 51, 53, 58, 98, 104, 106, 112, 115, 117, 119, 122, 123, 131, 136, 155
Herman, Dr. Judith 115, 116, 120
Hoffman, Brad 126
Houseal, Dr. 89
Husserl, Edmund 149

J

justified termination 16, 19, 64

L

Lakein, Alan 107

Lawless, Dr. Chuck 120
leadership development 28, 93, 94, 99, 125, 126, 127, 133
Leading with a Limp 121
Level of Education 44
Logical Investigations 149
Loving Someone with PTSD: A Biblical Guide to Understanding and Connecting with your Partner after Trauma 113

M
Maxwell, John 126
McConnel, Scot 89
Merkle, Dr. Benjamin 61
Mikkelsen, Robert 105
Miller, Dr. 8
misplaced leadership 79
mobbing effect 87, 88
Moustakas, Dr. Clark 150
Moving On – Moving Forward 132
Mueller, George 122

N
Northside Baptist Church 170

P
Pastoral Terminations: Common but often Avoidable 17
pastor's leadership style 17, 19, 20, 90, 91
Peacemaker: A Biblical Guide to Resolving Personal Conflict, The 111, 112
Peck, Kevin 126
Phenomenological Research Methods 150
phenomenology 149
poor people skills 17, 20, 90, 91
Post Traumatic Spiritual Stress Disorder (PTSSD) 38, 112, 115
Post-traumatic stress disorder (PTSD) 113
Powell, Thomas 37
Preventing Ministry Failure 37, 126

R
Ramsey, Dave 106
Recovery from Psychological Trauma 115
reentry into ministry 17, 54, 93, 94, 101, 110, 156
Roach, David 17, 90

S
Sande, Ken 111, 112
SBC Life 17, 20, 91
SBC Life's top reasons for unjustified terminations and resignations 17
   control issues 17
   pastor's leadership style being too strong 17
   pastor's leadership style being too weak 17
   poor people skills on the part of the pastor 17
   the church already being in conflict prior to the pastor's arrival 17
Size of Congregation 47
Southern Baptist 17, 90, 100, 152
Speight, Dr. Dallas 87, 96, 101, 150, 151, 152
Speight, Dr. Sheila 87, 96, 101, 150, 151, 152
Spiritual Disciplines for the Christian Life 123
spiritual healing 28, 93, 94, 99, 119, 120, 133
Spiritual Leadership 126
Spurgeon, Charles 122
Strange World of SBC 'Small' Churches, The 48
Surviving Friendly Fire: How to Respond When You are Hurt by Someone You Trust 121, 133

T
Tanner, Dr. Matthew 9, 11, 128, 170, 171
Tanner, Dr. Steve 8, 170

Tanner, Heather 8, 170
Tanner, Joshua 170
Tanner, Mary 8, 170
Tanner, Samantha 170
Tanner, Sammie 8
Tanner, Sarah 8, 170
Tanner, Shelby 8, 170
Thompson, David 10
Thompson, Steven H. 8, 9
Thornton, William 48
Time Away from Ministry 49, 50

U
unbiblical leadership structures 85

unjustified termination 15, 17, 19, 20, 54, 62, 67, 79, 85, 91, 100, 101, 120

V
Vessel, S.R. 87

W
Whitney, Dr. Don 123
Wickman, Chuck 38
Wilson, Michael Todd 126

Y
Years in Ministry 45

www.ingramcontent.com/pod-product-compliance
Lightning Source LLC
Chambersburg PA
CBHW020332170426
43200CB00006B/360